MICROSTATES IN WORLD AFFAIRS

MICROSTATES IN WORLD AFFAIRS

POLICY PROBLEMS AND OPTIONS

ELMER PLISCHKE

American Enterprise Institute for Public Policy Research
Washington, D.C.

Elmer Plischke is professor of government and politics at the University of Maryland.

Library of Congress Cataloging in Publication Data

Plischke, Elmer, 1914-
    Microstates in world affairs.

    (AEI studies ; 144)
    Includes bibliographical references.
    1. International relations. 2. Underdeveloped
areas—Foreign relations. I. Title. II. Series:
American Enterprise Institute for Public Policy
Research. AEI studies ; 144.
JX1395.P56   327   77-1351
ISBN 0-8447-3241-9

AEI Studies 144

Printed in the United States of America

This movement toward self-determination is one of the most powerful forces in twentieth century affairs. When the history of our era is finally written, it may prove to have been the most significant of all.

Henry A. Byroade
Assistant Secretary of State

Just as the concept of human liberty carried to its logical extreme would mean anarchy, so the principle of self-determination of peoples given unrestricted application could result in chaos.

Mrs. Franklin D. Roosevelt
U.S. Representative to the U.N. General Assembly

It appears desirable that a distinction be made between the right to independence and the question of full membership in the United Nations.

U Thant
Secretary General, United Nations

CONTENTS

PREFACE

The international community has expanded progressively during the past two centuries. Its growth pattern reflects waves of proliferation, usually accelerating following periods of widespread revolt and major war. The most impressive concomitants of United Nations practice in applying the principle of self-determination and in remolding the world community have been the remarkable quantitative growth and qualitative metamorphosis in the family of nations. In only three decades the spirit of what President John F. Kennedy called "a world-wide declaration of independence" has not only atomized expansive Western empires but also transformed more than 1.25 billion people, occupying nearly 14 million square miles of dependent territory, into approximately 90 new nations. As a result, by 1976, less than .03 percent of the world's landed domain, with under .05 percent of its population, remained as nonindependent residuum, which could be further segmented into some 50 to 100 or more additional "statelets."

Although the proliferation of states is transforming both the size and the nature of the family of nations, little attention has been devoted to assessing the consequences of this change to the international environment and to the policies of the United States and other powers. In the last decade, interest has been evoked only by such matters as small state proliferation, microstate membership in the United Nations, and concern with the internal and external affairs of a few specific smaller countries.

This survey is intended to provide a comprehensive analysis of the recent expansion of the global community and its possible and probable future growth. Some attention is paid to actual and hypothetical geographic factors, and particular emphasis is given to the diplomatic problems of the growing number of smaller countries—

especially the microstates—and to the problems engendered by them. The diplomatic relations studied here include direct bilateral representation through resident and other types of diplomatic missions, aspects of treaty-making and international conference attendance, and participation not merely in the United Nations but also in its specialized agencies and other selected global and regional intergovernmental organizations.

In addition to reviewing and refining factual findings, this analysis identifies problems, raises policy issues, and poses optional solutions for coping with them. It addresses, in essence, the fundamental dichotomy between people's aspirations toward self-determination, autonomous governance, independent statehood, and membership in the society of nations on the one hand and, on the other, the realities of diplomatic and international political viability—of the global community as well as of the individual nation-states. The policy task, in short, is one of coalescing, so far as possible, the rights of people to statehood, the rights of the eventuating states as integral components of the family of nations, and the rights of the community, as an aggregate, to sustain itself, to maintain its essential character, and to fulfill its established mission.

In his 1968 annual report, the secretary general of the United Nations indicated growing concern with sovereign entities which, as he put it, are exceptionally small in area, population, and human and economic resources. These have been called *small states, very small states, ministates,* and *microstates.* If a meaningful distinction is to be made, it would probably differentiate the *small* from what have generally come to be known as *ministates* and *microstates,* with the latter tending to be the preferred expression.

In a U.N. study, attention is devoted to "very small states and territories," having a population of 1 million or less (Jacques Rapoport, Ernest Muteba, and Joseph J. Therattil, *Small States and Territories: Status and Problems,* United Nations, Institute for Training and Research Series No. 3, New York: Arno Press, 1971). The same population delineation is used by William L. Harris for microstates ("Microstates in the United Nations: A Broader Purpose," *Columbia Journal of Transnational Law,* vol. 9, Spring 1970, p. 23).

On the other hand, in her study of "ministates and miniterritories," Patricia Wohlgemuth Blair limits population to 300,000 (*The Ministate Dilemma,* Carnegie Endowment for International Peace, Occasional Paper No. 6, rev. ed., New York: Carnegie Endowment, 1968, pp. 2–3). In a "Statistical Typology of Micro-States and Territories towards a Definition of a Micro-State," Charles L. Taylor notes the difficulties and arbitrariness involved in fixing an acceptable cutoff point and admits possibilities ranging from 100,000 to 1 million people (Annex to Rapoport, Muteba, and Therattil, *Small States and Territories*, pp. 183–202). Another author, Stanley A. de Smith, deems a territory or state to be "very small" if its population is less than 150,000 (*Microstates and Micronesia: Problems of America's Pacific Islands and Other Minute Territories*, New York: New York University Press, 1970, p. vii). This figure, some suggest, may become the minimum for U.N. membership.

In this analysis, for purposes of comparison and refinement, states and territories are grouped into ten population categories, as indicated in Chapter 2, with small states—under 5 million—divided into four groupings. Those states having less than 300,000 people are designated *microstates* and those with under 100,000 *submicrostates*. The use of a multiple population classification provides the advantage of encouraging contrastive and predictive analysis, even though emphasis may center primarily on the role of microstates in contemporary world affairs.

Population is the preferred criterion for categorizing nations and identifying microstates, and it is used as the primary factor in this inquiry. Territorial size, while discussed, is not employed as a determining standard, even though it has considerable correlation with population, especially for microstates. Nor are other possible distinguishing measures utilized, such as gross national product, trade, balance of payments, gold reserves, industrialization, resources, energy production and consumption, financial contribution level in the United Nations or other international organizations, and the like. If used as isolated determinants, they would prove to be rather meaningless, and, if combined in a complex formula, the result would deprive the analysis of the simplicity and purity of a single, readily comprehensible factor and would have less value in examining the smaller entities than the larger and more advanced powers.

Two hundred years ago, when the United States gained independence, the community of nations consisted of a small number of European imperial powers and a variety of smaller principalities. It might be questioned whether the newly emergent American republic of that time is not comparable to many of the small countries and microstates of the contemporary period, and whether much of this analysis, therefore, would not have been applicable to it. The manner of its emergence, its geographic separation from Europe, its unique nonconformist system of governance, and its relatively weak and uncertain status naturally affected its diplomatic posture and role.

Nevertheless, by current standards, the United States was relatively substantial in both territorial expanse and population size. Its original territory, consisting of roughly 800,000 square miles (based on the peace treaty of 1783), was larger than the continental domains of most European powers of that day, and exceeded that of all but a dozen contemporary states. Its early population size also compares favorably with the major countries of that era as well as with many states today. In 1790 the population of the United States numbered nearly 4 million. By 1800 it had increased by more than 1 million, so that its population was one-third as large as that of the British Isles. It exceeded that of the Netherlands and amounted to nearly one-fifth of that of the most populous European powers, except Russia. Furthermore, the United States then had a larger population than do half of the current members of the world community, and it was five times as populous as are nearly three dozen independent states today.

On a comparative basis, therefore, late in the eighteenth century the United States was by no means so diminutive as to cause or be encumbered by the representational problems now afflicting the family of nations. Because no universal diplomatic forum like the United Nations had yet been created, the principle of legal equality, regardless of population size, was not burdened with the ramifications of policy determination by democratic voting formulas and processes. The differences in the situation between the end of the nineteenth century and the post-World War II era, which are both qualitative and quantitative, have inspired this analysis.

1

INTRODUCTION

The growth of the family of nations has taken a remarkable turn since World War II. The prewar observer would have found strange indeed the emergence of an independent country of only 6,000 people occupying an isolated Pacific islet no larger than George Washington's estate, Mount Vernon. Or an Asian kingdom that became a member of the United Nations in 1971, pays but 0.02 percent of the U.N. budget, and appoints ambassadors to only two other countries. Or a newborn Caribbean country whose entire population would not fill the Rose Bowl and whose first envoy to the Organization of American States was a hired foreign national, yet wielding the same voting power in that organization as the United States. Or the U.N. scrutiny of the potential for independent nationhood of 1,600 islanders populating four square miles of Pacific coral atolls, to say nothing of the 92 people inhabiting the hermitic insular speck made famous by the *Bounty* mutineers in the eighteenth century.

Relations between nations have also taken odd twists, such as a miniature European Grand Duchy accrediting its own diplomatic emissaries to only ten other countries and relying on a neighbor to represent it to some fifty other governments. Or one country commissioning a single ambassador on multiple assignments to ten African states, and another government appointing nine ambassadors to represent it simultaneously to more than forty countries. Yet, all of these have occurred in recent years and reflect the debut of microstates in world affairs, a phenomenon as yet little understood.

It is well known that the relations of nations are constantly in flux, that nearly 100 new countries emerged in a single generation, and that the United Nations has virtually tripled in size since 1945. It is less well recognized, however, that the current momentum for

1

independence could well produce 50, 100 or even more new members in the global community in the years ahead. Or that even now, half of the members of the family of nations are less populous than the state of North Carolina, and that sixteen sovereign countries are smaller than such cities as Cartagena (Colombia) and Lubumbashi (Zaire). Or that four of every five American states are territorially larger than thirty independent countries. Or that, if the community of nations grew to 250 members, it is possible that close to half would have fewer people than metropolitan Peoria, Illinois, and some eighty countries could have smaller populations than the University of California.

Nor is it widely realized that the United States may be joined at sessions of the United Nations and global conferences by delegates from such states as Bahrain, Bhutan, Comoro, Grenada, the Maldives, Nauru, Qatar, São Tomé and Príncipe, Surinam, and Tonga. Or that self-determination has been discussed in the United Nations for exotic places like Afars and Issas, Belize, Brunei, Ifni, and Macao, as well as the Cayman, Cocos, and Tokelau islands, which are waiting in the wings. Or that if trends continue, nearly half of the world's nations could consist of islands and archipelagoes and two of every five would be microstates: fully sovereign nations with fewer than 300,000 people.

It is an axiom of international practice, but a legal fiction, that when a new state is born it becomes the legal equal of all others. The application of this concept in a community of dissimilar nations becoming even more so poses formidable difficulties. At present the United States is twice as populous as all of the existing small states (under 5 million) combined, and yet these account for more than half of the members of the global family and of the United Nations and can, therefore, control a majority of the voting power in important international institutions. More than half of the members of the United Nations individually contribute the minimum 0.02 percent of the budget and as a group pay less than one-sixteenth the share of the United States; but this group can muster a deciding majority vote in U.N. deliberations. If joined by a few additional low contributors—together paying only 2½ cents of each U.N. budget dollar—these mostly diminutive developing countries control a decisive two-thirds vote, and therefore can dominate U.N. decision making.[1]

---

[1] See the comments of Sydney D. Bailey in "U.N. Voting: Tyranny of the Majority?", *The World Today*, vol. 22 (June 1966), pp. 234-241; also see Chapter 7, section on "Financing and Voting," for several specific illustrations.

Change is characteristic not only of the interaction of peoples and their institutions but also of the study of such relations. One of these modifications involves the nature and quantity of international participants and how they are perceived. Criteria such as ethnicity, territory, politics, and legality were until recently applied to distinguish nations, and the nation-state was regarded as the principal, and at times even the sole, participator in world affairs.

As other categories of participation were delineated and came to play more and more influential roles, however, they attracted the attention of both policy makers and analysts. There have appeared, for example, increasing numbers of intergovernmental organizations, some of which possess highly developed structural systems and processes, semipublic and private international associations called nongovernmental organizations, multinational corporations whose operation and control have stimulated considerable national and international interest, and insurgent and other political action groups and mass movements that often transcend national frontiers and create problems for both individual states and the community of nations.

Perhaps the most consequential changes have occurred in the role of the quasi nations, including not only older entities like the traditional European principalities, Vatican City (Holy See), and new states that are in the process of formation but also those that have emerged but are unable to care for their own foreign policy and diplomatic relations or otherwise lack the full complement of qualities essential to statehood. A special feature of contemporary development, equally dramatic and important to the conduct and study of international affairs, is the creation of the substantial number of tiny new "statelets" that speckle the globe, producing new and sometimes strange problems in bilateral and multilateral relations.

The annals of the past abound with accounts of national avarice, separatist and secessionist movements, wars of independence, civil strife, crisis negotiations, and the acquisition, transfer, and loss of patrimony and population. Inherent for centuries in the hopes of mankind, the principle of self-determination enjoys widespread appeal; but only in recent decades has it generated a revolutionary impact on world affairs and contributed to remolding the composition of the community of nations. Central to this development have been the principles, institutions, and practices of the United Nations.

The framers of the United Nations Charter dealt with issues of governance, independence, and admission into statehood under three sets of stipulations about self-determination, the treatment of non-self-governing territories, and trusteeship. These were subsequently

3

liberalized and expanded under the precepts of decolonization, despite contentions by some governments that U.N. activism for such purposes contravened both the intention of its founders and Charter provisions specifically proscribing intervention in "matters which are essentially within the domestic jurisdiction" of states.[2] Nevertheless, the United Nations has assumed responsibility for trust territories, non-self-governing territories not under trusteeship, and strategic territories with small populations. It became apparent from the outset that the views and pressures of anticolonial powers were to prevail in both the General Assembly and the machinery it created to effect decolonization.

With each new U.N. member that had previously been a dependency or non-self-governing territory, the anticolonial powers strengthened their voice and increased their voting power. Former dependent entities, according to Assistant Secretary of State Henry A. Byroade, suffer a severe "colonial hangover," which assumes the form of intense and unreasonable suspicion of the policies and actions of Western nations, and fosters congenital opposition to them on world problems.[3] Sidney D. Bailey contends that, as the anticolonial forces increased, they were able to manage the majority decision-making system of the United Nations not only to get their way on many substantive questions but also to bend the rules to their advantage, thereby applying a democratic voting process against the colonial powers that had devised it, and rendering them the victims rather than the beneficiaries of procedural maneuvering.[4]

The noncolonial powers and former colonial territories have clearly been able to extend U.N. involvement and authority in decolonization matters. They have held countries possessing non-self-governing territory accountable to the United Nations for apparently ever-increasing reporting on the administration of such domains, and they have set up machinery to review and act upon the reports. They have ruled that the General Assembly, rather than the national government or the people themselves, is imbued with authority to determine when and how such territory achieves a "full measure of self-government," and that the United Nations has the right to proctor referenda on questions of decolonization. After gaining momentum, the anticolonial coalition has appeared to press for independence

---

[2] United Nations Charter, Article 2, paragraph 7.

[3] Henry A. Byroade, address on "The World's Colonies and Ex-Colonies: A Challenge to America," Department of State Press Release, no. 605 (October 30, 1953), p. 9.

[4] Bailey, "U.N. Voting: Tyranny of the Majority?", p. 234.

for the sake of independence—at the expense of the old colonial powers.[5] Although the positions of individual governments and the institutions of the United Nations may seem to be burdened with inconsistency sometimes bordering on schizophrenia, the drive for the extension of independence continues inexorably.[6] In dealing with the South African issue, over the years the United Nations adopted increasingly severe resolutions, and in 1976, despite its obligation to promote peace, it went so far as to endorse liberation movement action by any means, presumably including foreign military intervention.

The result is the creation not only of such substantial new countries as Burma, Indonesia, Kenya, Nigeria, and the Philippines but also the growing contingent of microstates. Having progressed through the Mideast, Africa, and South Asia, the self-determination/independence movement has come to focus largely on the remnants of empire—the remaining dependent island territories of the Caribbean and the Pacific. Draining the reservoir,[7] it could produce fifty to a hundred or more additional states, as discussed in Chapter 3. Many if not most of these are bound to be ministates, compounding the vicissitudes produced by this mercurial independence splurge.

One may wonder to what extent the drive of the United Nations has come to be prompted less by genuine concern with the equitable application of self-determination than by the deliberate policy of dismantling of the territories of colonial powers. Although the movement thus far has been directed at nonadjacent dependent territory and has not yet seriously affected contiguous continental domain, one

---

[5] But not against other imperial and newer colonial powers. For example, the United Nations has not taken action against the annexation of Estonia, Latvia, and Lithuania by the Soviet Union during World War II, a blatant denial of self-determination; nor has it intervened in such actions as the assumption of suzerainty in Tibet by Communist China, the absorption of Goa and Sikkim by India, the interposition of Morocco and other powers in the Spanish Sahara, and the annexation of Portuguese Timor by Indonesia, although the last of these is under consideration.

[6] It has been said that the United Nations probably would not condone certain actions by colonial powers today that were once allowed—or at least not contested. Jacques G. Rapoport, for example, questions whether the earlier acceptance by the United Nations of the changes in status of such territories as Puerto Rico, Greenland, the Netherlands Antilles, and Surinam, and the acquisition of American statehood by Alaska and Hawaii, would have been possible under U.N. policy and practices in the 1960s. See "The Participation of Ministates in International Affairs," *Proceedings of the American Society of International Law*, 1968, pp. 157-158.

[7] Roger Fisher declared as early as 1968 that decolonization had reached "the bottom of the barrel"; see "The Participation of Microstates in International Affairs," ibid., p. 165.

of the critical issues is whether the movement will terminate at the end of the current islet phase or move on toward the dismemberment of integral states. One might conjecture, in keeping with a more sanguine application of self-determination, that the next stage might involve separatism and secessionism as applied to island groups and even to contiguous territories and, if so, that the movement will continue to be directed primarily against the Western powers.[8]

The frenzy of fragmentation is producing a growing interest in the proliferation of small states and in their problems and their impact on the international community. Some published studies have dealt with the general growth of the family of nations and the development and role of individual small territories,[9] or with particular issues, such as the nature of statehood and the application of the dogma of sovereign equality.[10] A few analysts evidence concern with some of the broader aspects of the international position and difficulties of small states and territories,[11] or their relationship to basic

---

[8] Quincy Wright differentiates six interpretations of "self-determination"; see his commentary in ibid., pp. 187-188. For official U.S. statements on the principle of self-determination, see Walworth Barbour, "The Concept of Self-Determination in American Thought," *Department of State Bulletin*, vol. 31 (October 18, 1954), pp. 576-579; and Robert Murphy, "The Principle of Self-Determination in International Relations," *Department of State Bulletin*, vol. 33 (October 24, 1955), pp. 889-894. For additional commentary on the principle, see Rupert Emerson, "Self-Determination," *American Journal of International Law*, vol. 65 (July 1971), pp. 459-475; Elmer Plischke, "Self-Determination: Reflections on a Legacy," *World Affairs*, 1977, forthcoming issue; and Michla Pomerance, "Methods of Self-Determination and the Argument of 'Primitiveness,'" *Canadian Yearbook of International Law*, vol. 12 (1974), pp. 38-66. For an early survey of the post-World War II independence movement, see Elmer Plischke, "The Independence Boom," *Forum*, vol. 107 (May 1947), pp. 404-411.

[9] Michael M. Gunter, "Liechtenstein and the League of Nations: A Precedent for the United Nations' Ministate Problem?", *American Journal of International Law*, vol. 68 (July 1974), pp. 496-501; Josef L. Kunz, "The Status of the Holy See in International Law," *American Journal of International Law*, vol. 46 (April 1952), pp. 308-314; and de Smith, *Microstates and Micronesia*.

[10] For example, the historical survey of Robert A. Klein, *Sovereign Equality among States: The History of an Idea* (Downsview, Ontario: University of Toronto Press, 1974), and the short critical commentary of Ahmed Baba Miské, "Sovereign States Are Not Equal," *War/Peace Report* (April 1967), pp. 5-6.

[11] A symposium of essays is provided in Burton Benedict, ed., *Problems of Smaller Territories*, University of London, Institute of Commonwealth Studies (London: Athlone Press, 1967). See also David Vital, *The Inequality of States: A Study of the Small Powers in International Relations* (Oxford: Clarendon Press, 1967); and such shorter studies as G. Reid, *The Impact of Very Small Size on the International Behavior of Microstates* (Beverly Hills, Calif.: Sage Publications, 1974); S. A. de Smith, "Exceeding Small," chapter 5 in J. E. Fawcett and Rosalyn Higgins, eds., *International Organization* (Fair Lawn, N. J.: Oxford University Press, 1974), pp. 64-78; and Rapoport, "The Participation of Ministates in International Affairs," and Fisher, "The Participation of Microstates in International

questions of foreign policy behavior.[12] Most attention is devoted to the question of small-state membership in international organizations, especially the United Nations. The process and consequences of decolonization, central to the reshaping of the community of nations since World War II, attract considerable interest.[13] Literature concerned with microstate membership only surfaced, however, following the admission of the Maldives by the United Nations. Two comprehensive surveys of the problems and potentialities of microentity proliferation, affiliation, and status were published in the late 1960s.[14]

Affairs," *Proceedings of the American Society of International Law*, 1968, pp. 155-163, 164-188.

[12] See Maurice A. East, "Size and Foreign Policy Behavior: A Test of Two Models," *World Politics*, vol. 25 (July 1973), pp. 556-576, which analyzes and compares methods of large and small state behavior; and Chadwick F. Alger and Steven J. Brams, "Patterns of Representation in National Capitals and Intergovernmental Organizations," *World Politics*, vol. 19 (July 1967), pp. 646-663. Other books dealing with small size and foreign relations behavior include David Vital, *The Survival of Small States* (New York: Oxford University Press, 1971); and August Schou and Arne O. Brundtland, eds., *Small States in International Relations* (New York: Wiley Interscience, 1971). For a study of small state voting behavior in the United Nations that indicates a high degree of cohesiveness on colonial and economic questions, see Joseph R. Harbert, "The Behavior of the Ministates in the United Nations, 1971-1972," *International Organization*, vol. 30 (Winter 1976), pp. 109-127.

[13] The following are merely representative of the literature on decolonization: Maurice Barbier, *Le Comité de Décolonisation des Nations Unis* (The Hague: Nijhoff, 1974); Lord Caradon, "Vanishing Colonies: The Thirty Years That Changed the World," *The Interdependent* (July/August 1975), pp. 49-51; Harrison G. Gough and Guiseppe de Palma, "Attitudes toward Colonialism, Political Dependence, and Independence," *Journal of Psychology*, vol. 60 (1965), pp. 155-163; Nancy L. Hoepli, ed., *The Afermath of Colonialism*, vol. 45, no. 1 (New York: Reference Shelf, 1973); Harold Karan Jacobson, "The United Nations and Colonialism: A Tentative Appraisal," *International Organization*, vol. 16 (Winter 1962), pp. 37-56; David A. Kay, "The Politics of Decolonization: The New Nations and the United Nations Political Process," *International Organization*, vol. 21 (Autumn 1967), pp. 786-811; and Yassin El-Ayouty's more specialized study, *The United Nations and Decolonization: The Role of Afro-Asia* (The Hague: Nijhoff, 1971).

[14] Patricia Wohlgemuth Blair, *The Ministate Dilemma*, Carnegie Endowment for International Peace, Occasional Paper No. 6, rev. ed. (New York: Carnegie Endowment, 1968); and Jacques Rapoport, Ernest Muteba, and Joseph J. Therattil, *Small States and Territories: Status and Problems*, United Nations Institute for Training and Research Series No. 3 (New York: Arno Press, 1971). Systematic background information on states and other political units is provided in J. David Singer and Melvin Small, "The Composition and Status Ordering of the International System, 1815-1940," *World Politics*, vol. 18 (January 1966), pp. 236-282; Bruce M. Russet, J. David Singer, and Melvin Small, "National Political Units in the Twentieth Century: A Standardized List," *American Political Science Review*, vol. 62 (September 1968), pp. 932-951; and Melvin Small and J. David Singer, "The Diplomatic Importance of States, 1816-1970," *World Politics*, vol. 25 (July 1973), pp. 577-599.

Other studies, including a few that antedated the microstate era,[15] were undertaken to examine the more limited question of U.N. membership and to suggest ways of dealing with it,[16] or specifically to scrutinize such issues as apportionment and voting authority.[17]

This study is concerned with the nature, status, and problems of small states—particularly the microstates—as members of the international community. It reviews the progress of their proliferation and their aggregate role as an important and expanding component of the family of nations. It also projects their potential increase and examines possible geopolitical consequences to the global community, including quantitative analysis of their location and insular status. It does not address the essence, propriety, or theoretical cogency of such matters as nation building and statehood, colonialism and decolonization, integration and disintegration, social and cultural values, internal and external economic needs and viability, governmental systems and modernization, or political leadership and national stability.

The investigation is focused on those facets of the international environment in which the diminutive states, like other powers, function and are expected to deport themselves as individual and collective participants. It examines selected aspects of the microstates' engagement in diplomatic representation to and among other states, their treaty making, their involvement in multipartite conferences,

---

[15] Such as Royden J. Dangerfield, "The United States, the United Nations, and the Emerging Nations," *American Government Annual, 1963-1964* (New York: Holt, Rinehart and Winston, 1963), pp. 131-155; Annette Baxter Fox, "Small States of Western Europe in the United Nations," *International Organization*, vol. 19 (Summer 1965), pp. 774-786; and Andrew D. Sens, "Newly Independent States, the United Nations and Some Thoughts on the Nature of the Development Process," *Journal of Politics*, vol. 30 (February 1968), pp. 114-136.

[16] William M. Harris, "Microstates in the United Nations: A Broader Purpose," *Columbia Journal of Transnational Law*, vol. 9 (Spring 1970), pp. 23-53; David A. Kay, *The New Nations in the United Nations, 1960-1967* (New York: Columbia University Press, 1970); Stephen M. Schwebel, "Ministates and a More Effective United Nations," *American Journal of International Law*, vol. 67 (January 1973), pp. 108-116; and Urban Whitaker, "Proliferation in the U.N.: Mini-Membership for Mini-States," *War/Peace Report* (April 1967), pp. 3-5.

[17] These include such analyses as Richard N. Gardner, "United Nations Procedures and Power Realities: The International Apportionment Problem," *Department of State Bulletin*, vol. 52 (May 10, 1965), pp. 701-711; and Catherine Senf Manno, "Selective Weighted Voting in the U.N. General Assembly: Rationale and Methods," *International Organization*, vol. 20 (Winter 1966), pp. 37-62. Critiques of the weighted voting process are to be found in such articles as Bailey's "U.N. Voting: Tyranny of the Majority?", and T. T. B. Koh, "Microstates and the New U.N. Majority," *The Interdependent* (July/August 1975), pp. 88-89.

and their membership in the United Nations and other international organizations. It concentrates on determining facts about their low level of participation in these processes and institutions, the difficulties they experience, and the problems they engender for other countries and the international community. Except where otherwise noted, statistical information contained in this analysis is computed as of January 1976.

The study suggests alternative methods of bilateral diplomatic exchange and affiliation with international agencies. It raises considerations of political responsibility for effective functioning within the diplomatic community, and of possible effects of the limited involvement and contribution of small states. It considers potential intensification of difficulties as more microstates emerge as sovereign entities. In sum, without prescribing solutions, it poses questions that need to be faced and resolved by national and international policy makers from the perspectives of the corporate family of nations, the international organizations, the United States, and other powers in treating the microstate malady.

Politics may make strange bedfellows. International politics appears to be producing a heterogeneous if not aberrant global fraternity—"dispensing," to paraphrase Plato, "a sort of equality to equals and unequals alike." The central question is not whether peoples are entitled to manage their own affairs and enjoy political independence, but whether, irrespective of their size and ability to fulfill their responsibilities, they should also be entitled to sovereign equality in the affairs of the community of nations.

The primary alternative to halting an escalating rush to independence and global status by many minute territories is to disestablish the concept of legal equality as a fundamental characteristic of both statehood and membership in the community of nations, or at least as an automatic avenue to international status and participation. Equal status has so long been regarded as an integral quality of statehood, however, that efforts to establish alternative concepts may well prove fruitless. The only practical alternative, therefore, may be to retard and manage the future proliferation of states and to delimit microstate participation in global forums and affairs.

The United States and other powers need to examine, and soon, how unchecked proliferation of Lilliputian nations is likely to affect the existing international system and whether the transformation can be endured by the individual states and the collective community. Already the problem threatens to get out of hand. The longer action is delayed, the fewer the options that will be available to responsible powers for amelioration or resolution of the problem, and the more difficult it will be to make a firm stand against the momentum, bring proliferation under control, and undo the damage that has been perpetrated.

2
THE COMMUNITY OF NATIONS

Never stable, the community of nations is today particularly prone to fragmentation. Even as states appear to be groping toward cooperation, if not coalescence, through integrative movements and institutions, splinter movements have become rampant in world affairs and new participants proliferate. The lure of independence and sovereignty is great and seems on occasion to override the qualities of viability and welfare necessary for modern statehood.

Few of the present states have enjoyed any great longevity. Although the international community has been expanding for two centuries—with new states emerging in waves following major wars and during periods of revolution and the disintegration of empires—a compelling majority of its current members are recent creations. Despite their common denominator of legal equality, states of course differ considerably—in homogeneity, social and cultural development, political stability, population and territorial size, agricultural and mineral resources, degree of industrialization, standard of living, commerce and balance of payments, and in their sense of responsibility toward the world community.

Quantitative Trends

In 1976 the family of nations consisted of 155 states.[1] This figure reflects contemporary international practice, without attempting to

---

[1] This figure applies as of January 1976 and reflects the listing of states contained in Appendix A, which is used as the basis of tabulation in this study. The two Vietnams, though subsequently united, are separately included in Appendix A, and new states created in 1976, such as the Seychelles (a microstate) and Transkei, are not. Recent changes, however, produce little effect on basic computations and trends.

define the theoretical essence of statehood. It includes not only those states deemed to be independent in the traditional sense but also a few otherwise questionable entities that satisfy two or more of four criteria: (1) acknowledgment of independence by the former parent or colonial country; (2) formal recognition by some other states; (3) establishment and maintenance of regularized bilateral diplomatic relations with one or more governments; and (4) membership (other than observership) in the United Nations or its specialized agencies.

The list of existing nations (presented in Appendix A) therefore includes Bhutan, Byelorussia, the Ukraine, and Vatican City (Holy See). It encompasses such small islands and archipelagoes as the Bahamas, the Maldives, Nauru, São Tomé and Príncipe, Tonga (Friendly Islands), and Western Samoa, all of which are microstates, and also the newer countries (1973–1975)—Angola, Cape Verde Islands, Comoro Islands,[2] Grenada, Guinea-Bissau, Mozambique, Papua New Guinea, and Surinam (Dutch Guiana), and the "duo-states"—the two Chinas, Germanies, Koreas, and Yemens.

On the other hand, the list does not include the long-time European principalities (Andorra, Liechtenstein, Monaco, and San Remo [3]), potentially separatist territories (Sikkim [4] and Zanzibar [5]), and certain former states (Estonia, Latvia, and Lithuania). The list also omits colonial areas that at the end of 1976 either appeared to be on the verge of independence (Antigua,[6] the Azores,[7] and Belize/British

[2] In 1974 the French government promised orderly transition to independence in 1978 to the Comoro Archipelago. In the interim, when the preponderant majority on three of the four islands voted for independence, President Ahmed Abdallah proclaimed independence for the entire group. Officials of one of four islands (Mayette), however, supported by a majority of its voters, wished to remain French. Abdallah was overthrown in a bloodless coup and pro-French leaders took control of the island group and requested French recognition of independence, subject to maintaining close ties with Paris. The Comoro Chamber of Deputies declared the country's independence on July 6, 1975.

[3] Despite the fact that, except for Andorra, they are members of selected U.N. specialized agencies and participate in international treaty making and conferences, as noted below.

[4] Formerly an Indian protectorate, Sikkim was annexed by India as an associate state in 1974, and its monarchy was abolished in 1975.

[5] Formerly independent, Zanzibar became part of Tanzania in 1964.

[6] Antigua was granted semi-independence in 1967, as an associate member of the British Commonwealth, with London handling its external affairs and defense. In 1975, Antigua's major political parties pressed for complete independence.

[7] The Azores (and Madeira) were granted greater regional autonomy by Portugal late in 1975. The independence problem of the Azores is unique in that pressure for independence is not a traditional conflict of native islanders against the colonial power, but rather a movement to be freed from a particular type of

Honduras [8]), or had recently been involved in serious independence disputes (South West Africa/Namibia,[9] Portuguese Timor,[10] Southern Rhodesia,[11] and the Spanish Sahara [12]).

One of the most obvious and impressive contemporary factors in the world community is its expansion since World War II. The list of nations has more than tripled in number in the twentieth century and has increased by nearly 150 percent since 1940.[13] This

---

metropolitan political leadership. A coalition of several independence groups has actively opposed potential leftist leadership in Portugal.

[8] Belize (British Honduras) was granted internal self-government by Britain in 1964. Its inhabitants hesitate to become independent in fear of invasion and absorption by Guatemala.

[9] South West Africa, for years a German protectorate, was surrendered to South Africa in 1915 and was administered as a League of Nations mandate, but after World War II South Africa refused to accept U.N. trusteeship over the territory. In 1968 the U.N. General Assembly created a council to administer the territory and renamed it Namibia. The Security Council condemned South Africa in 1970 for maintaining illegal hegemony in the area, and the following year the International Court of Justice, in an advisory opinion, declared South Africa to be occupying the territory illegally. A multiracial conference, under South African sponsorship but excluding the local faction recognized by the United Nations, plans independence for Namibia at the end of December 1978. Meanwhile, the United Nations has demanded immediate elections under its supervision. Eventual independence appears to be a certainty, but the struggle for control portends possible guerrilla warfare.

[10] When Portuguese Timor was promised independence by Lisbon, factions fought for political control, civil war drove the Portuguese administration from the island in 1975, and refugees fled into Western Timor (part of Indonesia). The Indonesian government intervened and in July 1976 it formally annexed the territory.

[11] In 1965 the Rhodesian government unilaterally declared its independence, which the British government refused to acknowledge, and the United Nations imposed economic sanctions on the territory. Later, in 1968, the Security Council ordered a trade embargo, and in 1970 Rhodesia proclaimed a new constitution to establish the territory as a republic. Rhodesia's conflict has been less one of achieving independence from Britain than a struggle for leadership and control over the territory as an independent country, and negotiations were launched in 1976 to provide for a system of majority rule.

[12] Spain decided in 1975 to withdraw from the Spanish Sahara and grant independence subject to a plebiscite monitored by the United Nations. But local groups contended for control, a struggle complicated by the intervention of three African powers—Algeria supporting the Spanish proposal for the referendum and independence, but Morocco and Mauritania demanding that the territory be ceded to them. Late in 1975 Morocco launched a "march of conquest" by 350,000 unarmed civilians to dramatize its claim to sovereignty. The marchers were withdrawn when the Spanish government enacted a decolonization law ending its rule and establishing a joint interim administration pending the division of the territory between Morocco and Mauritania.

[13] See Appendix A for independence dates. In 1940 there were sixty-four states; see Table 2B. This figure includes the Vatican, but not Byelorussia and the Ukraine or the Baltic states of Estonia, Latvia, and Lithuania. The list of ninety-

13

growth represents a fairly constant annual increment, except for a few years in the early 1940s, the early 1950s, and 1969. Sixteen states joined the global community in the five years immediately following World War II, largely in the Asian area.[14] The United States launched the initial wave of the independence boom by granting international statehood to the Philippines on July 4, 1946—the first colonial, non-mandated territory to gain independence. By far the largest expansion occurred in the 1960s, however, when forty-four new states emerged —nearly three-fourths of which lie in sub-Saharan Africa.[15] While the growth rate subsequently declined, it nevertheless remains substantial, with seventeen states joining the international community between 1970 and 1975, and two more in 1976.[16]

Expansion is likely to continue as a consequence of the United Nations' insistence on self-determination for dependent territories. The growing drive for decolonization, unleashed within the United Nations under the guise of the traditional American policy supporting self-government, and augmented as dependent territories join with former colonies and other anticolonial forces in determining collective international practice, is bound to continue fragmentation for some time, as discussed in the next chapter.

Changing Geographic Complexion

More important than simple aggregate growth is the post-World War II change in the basic geographic composition of the society of

one states that have joined the family of nations since 1940 includes Bhutan, Byelorussia and the Ukraine, and the newer states (for the period 1970 to 1976, see footnote 16).

[14] Iceland, Lebanon, and Syria emerged during World War II (1943-1944). Beginning with Jordan, Korea, and the Philippines in 1945 and 1946, the rate of expansion increased each year during this half decade, with six new states created in 1949. Aside from the German Democratic Republic, there were two in the Mideast (Israel and Jordan) and thirteen in Asia, the Indian Ocean, and the Western Pacific (including Indonesia, the Philippines, and Ceylon/Sri Lanka).

[15] The African increment numbered thirty-one. The others included four in the Western Hemisphere, three in the Mideast and North Africa, and two each in Europe, Asia/Indian Ocean, and Oceania.

[16] Angola, Bahamas, Bahrain, Bangladesh, Cape Verde Islands, Comoro Islands, Fiji, Grenada, Guinea-Bissau, Mozambique, Oman, Papua New Guinea, Qatar, Surinam, São Tomé and Príncipe, Tonga, and the United Arab Emirates. Six of these are located in the African area, four in the Mideast/North Africa, three in the Western Hemisphere as well as in Oceania, and one in Asia. Those that became independent in 1976 include the Seychelles and Transkei.

14

nations, wrought primarily by concentrations of new states in former colonial areas and by the proliferation of island-states.[17] When the United States proclaimed its independence two centuries ago, the world diplomatic community centered almost entirely in Europe. The young American government, like many emergent states, developed its diplomatic community selectively and gradually.[18] In the first four decades following the Revolution, it established diplomatic relations with only eight European powers,[19] and five more during the next two decades.[20] Following the revolt of a number of Latin American colonies in the first quarter of the nineteenth century, diplomatic relations also were established with them. After sixty years the United States had exchanged diplomatic missions with merely two dozen countries in Europe and the Western Hemisphere.[21] Relations also were commenced with five Oriental and Pacific states [22] and with four governments in the Mideast and Africa by the 1880s.[23]

At the turn of the century, having converted to a program of universal diplomatic exchange, the United States maintained relations with some forty countries—eighteen in the Western Hemisphere, sixteen in Europe, and eight in other areas. At this time, only 20 percent of the independent countries lay outside of Europe and the Western Hemisphere. The wave of new states that emerged following World War I embraced three British Dominions [24] and a number of Baltic and other East European countries, but this merely reinforced

---

[17] The geographic area allocation used in this analysis, as specified in Appendix A and elsewhere, comports with the geographic breakdown utilized in the United Nations *Statistical Yearbook, 1974* (1975) and the U.S. Department of State's *Issues: World Data Handbook* (1972), as augmented, where necessary, on the basis of areal proximity.

[18] For analysis of the historical development of American diplomatic relations, including some review of the waves of increase, see Elmer Plischke, *United States Diplomats and Their Missions: A Profile of American Diplomatic Emissaries since 1778* (Washington, D.C.: American Enterprise Institute, 1975), especially Chapter 1, Table 1, and Appendix Tables A-1 and A-2.

[19] England, France, the Netherlands, Portugal, Prussia, Russia, Spain, and Sweden.

[20] Denmark (1827), Belgium (1832), the Two Sicilies (1832), Austria-Hungary (1838), and Italy (1840). Switzerland was added in 1853.

[21] By 1850, they numbered twenty-seven, including the Holy See and Texas (which joined the Union in 1845) and counting the five Central American republics (Costa Rica, El Salvador, Guatemala, Honduras, and Nicaragua) as separate entities.

[22] China (1844), Hawaii (1853), and Japan (1859); later followed by Siam/Thailand (1882) and Korea (1883).

[23] Turkey (1831), Egypt (1849), Liberia (1864), and Persia/Iran (1883).

[24] Canada (U.S. commenced diplomatic relations in 1927), Ireland (1927), and South Africa (1930).

the basic geographic structure of the international community. In 1940 there were sixty-four nations,[25] three-fourths of which were located in Europe and the Western Hemisphere, as shown in Table 1.

In the years following World War II, and especially since 1960, geographic patterning changed markedly. Major increases in the number of independent countries occurred in Africa, Asia (including the Indian Ocean), and the Mideast/North African area. While only thirteen additional states were established in the Western Hemisphere and Europe combined,[26] fifteen emerged in the Middle East and North Africa, thirty-nine in sub-Saharan Africa, nineteen in Asia and the Indian Ocean, and five in Oceania (Table 1). The areal allocation of nations reversed after World War II in that by 1976, 60 percent of the community of nations lay outside the Western Hemisphere and Europe. During the post-World War II era the number of states in the Mideast and North Africa increased by 350 percent (from six to twenty-one), by 480 percent in Asia and the Indian Ocean basin (from five to twenty-four), and by 1,400 percent in sub-Saharan Africa (from three to forty-two). Today the largest number of nations is to be found in sub-Saharan Africa, followed by Europe, the Western Hemisphere, Asia, the Middle East/North Africa, and Oceania (Table 1). Postwar transformations have thus altered drastically the global political role of the non-European and non-Western Hemisphere geographic areas.

Until World War II the preponderant majority of states were located on the continents. Of the few nineteenth century countries that were island-states, five continue as members of the current international community—the United Kingdom, Japan, and three Caribbean countries, Cuba, the Dominican Republic, and Haiti.[27] Ireland and New Zealand were added after World War I,[28] and by 1940 this

---

[25] Only a few independent states went out of existence during this century and a half—notably Hawaii, Korea, Montenegro, the Two Sicilies, and Texas, which were superseded or annexed by other states. Korea was later revived. Were Estonia, Latvia, and Lithuania, occupied by Soviet forces in June 1940 and absorbed by the Soviet Union, to be included, the ratio for Europe would be higher; they are incorporated neither in this total nor in Appendix A and derivative tables.

[26] Western Hemisphere: Guyana, Surinam, and five Caribbean island countries; Europe: Cyprus, East Germany, Iceland, and Malta, plus the two Soviet republics—Byelorussia and the Ukraine—despite their limited international status and activities.

[27] For a time Hawaii and the Two Sicilies also belonged to the group of nineteenth century island-states.

[28] In view of its continental size, Australia is not included as an island-state.

16

Table 1

PAST AND POTENTIAL INCREASE OF INDEPENDENT NATIONS

Geographic Area [a]	Total Nations, 1940		1940–75 Increase (number)	Total Nations, 1975		Potential Increase [b] (number)	Potential Total	
	Number	Percent of total		Number	Percent of total		Number	Percent of total
Western Hemisphere	22	34.4	7	29	18.7	31	60	19.7
Europe	26	40.6	6	32	20.6	23	55	18.0
Mideast and North Africa	6	9.4	15	21	13.6	4	25	8.2
Sub-Saharan Africa	3	4.7	39	42	27.1	6	48	15.7
Asia and Indian Ocean	5	7.8	19	24	15.5	23	47	15.4
Oceania	2	3.1	5	7	4.5	46	53	17.4
Polar regions	0	0	0	0	0	17	17	5.6
Total	64	100.0	91	155	100.0	150	305	100.0

a Based on Appendix A. The figure for Europe includes the Soviet Union together with Byelorussia and the Ukraine; the Mideast and North Africa includes Iran, the Sudan, and Turkey; sub-Saharan Africa includes the Cape Verde Islands, Comoro Islands, Mauritius, and São Tomé/Príncipe; Asia and the Indian Ocean includes Bhutan, Indonesia, the Maldives, the Philippines, and Sri Lanka; and Australia, New Zealand, and Papua New Guinea are included in Oceania.

b See Appendix B for a list of these potential additions.

Source: Appendix A and Appendix B.

group of seven island-states constituted approximately one-tenth of the society of nations. The ratio has since doubled, beginning with Iceland becoming independent in 1944, the Philippines two years later, and Ceylon and Indonesia in the late 1940s. The greatest change occurred from 1960 to 1975, however, when nineteen additional island-states emerged, raising the total to thirty. Most of the expansion after 1940 took place in the Caribbean (five states), the Indian Ocean (five), and the Pacific and Oceania (eight),[29] and many of these new insular states are small in terms of both population and geographic size—perhaps portending future developments.

Proliferation of Small Countries and Microstates

Another even more critical change in the family of nations is the increasing number of small countries and microstates emerging as participants in world affairs. The members of the community of nations may be classified in various population categories. Ten such groupings are employed in Tables 2A and 2B and elsewhere (based on Appendix A), as follows: [30]

	Microstates		Medium States
A	Under 100,000	E	5,000,000-25,000,000
B	100,000-300,000	F	25,000,000-50,000,000
	Small States		Large States
C	300,000-1,000,000	G	50,000,000- 75,000,000
D	1,000,000-5,000,000	H	75,000,000-100,000,000
		I	100,000,000-200,000,000
		J	More than 200,000,000

---

[29] The others are located in the eastern Atlantic and the Mediterranean Sea, but these areas seem less likely to be very fertile sites for the production of additional island-states.

[30] Micro, small, medium, and large are of course relative concepts, so the results of analysis based on this population breakdown may at times be arbitrary. It should also be kept in mind that states change in population and therefore move from category to category, and that the categorizations given represent the current situation or relative relationship and are subject to minor variation from year to year. Nevertheless, the broader generalizations and trends revealed in this analysis are less ephemeral and can be important to understanding the current and future composition and interrelations of the community of nations.

Category A states, representing the smallest population class, are sometimes referred to as submicrostates. The current microstates (with date of independence and population category) are:

Bahamas (1973)	B	Maldives (1965)	B
Bahrain (1971)	B	Nauru (1968)	A
Barbados (1966)	B	Qatar (1971)	B
Cape Verde Islands		São Tomé and Príncipe	
(1975)	B	(1975)	A
Comoro Islands (1975)	B	Tonga (1970)	A
Equatorial Guinea (1968)	B	United Arab Emirates	
		(1971)	B
Grenada (1974)	A	Vatican City (——)	A
Iceland (1944)	B	Western Samoa (1962)	B

The Seychelles (category A) was added to this group in 1976.

As of 1976 only four countries exceeded 200 million in population,[31] two had more than 100 million,[32] and seven others had 50 million or more.[33] Six of these thirteen most populous states are Asian and four are European; six came into existence since World War II. Among the medium-sized countries, thirteen have populations ranging from 25 to 50 million. Thus, only twenty-six states, or one in six, represent the five largest population categories (25 million and up in population). Although another fifty of the medium-sized states range from 5 to 25 million, less than half (49 percent) of the current members of the community of nations have populations exceeding 5 million —approximately the population of metropolitan Philadelphia.[34]

Of the smaller countries, forty-seven (30 percent of the total) range from 1 to 5 million people, including nineteen in sub-Saharan Africa[35] and eleven in the Western Hemisphere,[36] but also including New Zealand and such European countries as Denmark, Finland, Ireland, and Norway. Even more significant, thirty-two countries, one-fifth of the members of the contemporary international community,

---

[31] Chinese People's Republic, India, the Soviet Union, and the United States.

[32] Indonesia and Japan.

[33] Bangladesh, Brazil, the Federal Republic of Germany, Italy, Nigeria, Pakistan, and the United Kingdom.

[34] Sixteen of the largest cities of the world are reported to have populations exceeding 5 million: Bombay, Buenos Aires, Calcutta, Chicago, London, Los Angeles, Mexico City, Moscow, New York, Osaka, Paris, Peking, São Paulo (Brazil), Seoul, Shanghai, and Tokyo.

[35] Liberia and eighteen of the post-1940 states.

[36] Three South American (Bolivia, Paraguay, and Uruguay), five Central American, and three Caribbean states (Haiti, Jamaica, and the Dominican Republic).

Table 2

INDEPENDENT NATIONS BY POPULATION CATEGORY

Geographic Area	Micro			Small			Medium			Large					Total	Per-cent	Insular States
	A	B	Total	C	D	Total	E	F	Total	G	H	I	J	Total			
PART A																	
Western Hemisphere	1	2	3	3	11	14	9	1	10	0	1	0	1	2	29	19	8
Europe	1	1	2	3	5	8	14	4	18	3	0	0	1	4	32	21	5
Mideast and North Africa	0	3	3	2	6	8	7	3	10	0	0	0	0	0	21	14	0
Sub-Saharan Africa	1	3	4	7	19	26	10	1	11	1	0	0	0	1	42	27	5
Asia and Indian Ocean	0	1	1	0	4	4	9	4	13	2	0	2	2	6	24	15	6
Oceania	2	1	3	1	2	3	1	0	1	0	0	0	0	0	7	4	6
Total	5	11	16	16	47	63	50	13	63	6	1	2	4	13	155	100	30
PART B																	
Pre-1940	1	0		1	18		28	9		3	1	1	2		64	41	
Post-1940	4	11		15	29		22	4		3	0	1	2		91	59	
Total	5	11		16	47		50	13		6	1	2	4		155	100	

Source: Appendix A.

have less than 1 million people,[37] and half of these—the microstates —are under 300,000.[38]

The most noteworthy trend in the recent growth of the international community is the remarkable increase, both relative and absolute, in the number of smaller states. Table 2 indicates that while twenty (31 percent) of the sixty-four pre-World War II states were under 5 million in population, some fifty-nine (65 percent) of the ninety-one post-1940 states fall into this grouping, doubling the ratio. Put another way, only one of three pre-World War II states fall below this population level while the postwar addition amounts to nearly two of three, and, combined, small states came to constitute more than half of the participants in the international community.[39]

Also significant is the fact that, except for Vatican City, which enjoys a unique role, all of the microstates are post-World War II creations, and they now account for 10 percent of the world's independent states. All except Iceland came into being after 1960, and nine of them joined the family of nations in the 1970s, evidencing the present trend toward proliferation of tiny nation-states. Equally worthy of note, five (or one-third) are actually submicrostates, with populations under 100,000—the size of dozens of cities in the United States, or of enrollments in at least two American universities, or of the attendance at some major sports events. Another factor to be considered is the geographic dispersion of the sixteen microstates. They are least prevalent in Asia and Europe. Most microstates are islands and archipelagoes [40] located primarily in the Caribbean, the

---

[37] Eleven in sub-Saharan Africa, five each in the Western Hemisphere, Europe, and the Mideast/North Africa, and the rest in Asia and Oceania. By comparison, thirty-four cities in the United States are more populous than these countries.

[38] They are equally distributed, with generally two or three in each of the six basic geographic areas. More than 110 American cities exceed these countries in population size. For example, Lancaster, Pennsylvania (320,000), and Columbia, South Carolina (323,000), reportedly have more population than Iceland or Malta and are nearly as populous as Luxembourg. Nearly 250 American cities have populations exceeding 100,000 and are therefore larger than any of the submicrostates.

[39] By comparison, in 1970 twelve of the American states exceeded 5 million in population, making them larger than half of the members of the family of nations. Only fourteen American states have under 1 million population, and no American state has under 300,000. Three American states in four have more than 1 million and thus are more populous than thirty-two countries, one-fifth of the members of the community of nations.

[40] Among the microstates only the Vatican, three Mideast oil countries, and Equatorial Guinea are not island-states. Of the thirty insular states mentioned earlier, twenty-three (77 percent) are small in population, sixteen of them under 1 million; eleven are microstates.

Indian Ocean, the Pacific, and Oceania, which suggests a considerable potential for future proliferation.

Although the ratio of population to geographic size (population density) is critical to the economic and social development of states, and might be assumed to be of less importance to their participation in the diplomatic world, a few comments and comparisons may be useful. In geographic area, as noted in Appendix A, states vary in size from such tiny entities as Vatican City (0.17 square miles) and the island of Nauru (8 square miles) to the sizable continental powers —including Australia (2,968,000 square miles), Brazil (3,286,500), the United States (3,628,200), the People's Republic of China (3,691,500), Canada (3,851,800), and the Soviet Union (8,647,300). Two other states, Argentina and India, exceed 1 million square miles.[41] Except for Australia, Argentina, and Canada, these countries also have large populations (over 50 million). On the other hand, the territory of three countries having populations between 50 and 75 million— Bangladesh, the Federal Republic of Germany, and the United Kingdom—is under 100,000 square miles.[42]

As might be expected, greater consistency in correlating geographic size and population is to be found among the microstates. Nine of the sixteen are under 1,000 square miles,[43] and all of them are under 5,000 square miles,[44] except for Equatorial Guinea (10,800 square miles), the United Arab Emirates (32,000 square miles), and Iceland (39,700 square miles). Fourteen other small states (under 5 million) are less than 10,000 square miles,[45] and four of these are under 1,000 square miles.[46] Thus, thirty (or 38 percent) of the seventy-nine states classified as small in population (under 5 million) are also among the smaller states in geographic size.[47] On the

---

[41] Other sizable states—larger than 500,000 square miles—include Mongolia (604,200), Iran (636,400), Libya (679,500), Indonesia (735,300), Mexico (761,600), Saudi Arabia (873,000), Zaire (905,100), Algeria (920,000), and the Sudan (967,500). Of these, only Indonesia has a large population. Libya and Mongolia have small populations numbering less than 2.5 million.

[42] This is roughly the territorial size of Colorado. Eight American states exceed 100,000 square miles—Alaska, Arizona, California, Colorado, Montana, Nevada, New Mexico, and Texas—each of which, territorially, is larger than eighty-seven independent countries, or 56 percent of the community of nations.

[43] This is less than the size of Rhode Island, the smallest of the American states.

[44] Approximately the size of Connecticut, the third smallest American state.

[45] Roughly the size of Maryland. Territorially, the largest of these are El Salvador, Fiji, Israel, and Kuwait.

[46] Luxembourg (999), Malta (122), Mauritius (787), and Singapore (225).

[47] By comparison, forty-two (or 84 percent) of the fifty American states exceed these thirty small independent countries in geographic size.

other hand, twenty-one of the less populous states have territories exceeding 100,000 square miles,[48] more than half of which are located in Africa, and all but seven of which have gained independence since World War II.

All but three of the thirty territorially small states are post-1940 creations,[49] evidencing a now-recognizable expansionary trend in the number of states that are small not only in population but also in geographic size. One obvious conclusion is that small territories seeking independence and statehood are also likely to have small populations, and that neither their population nor their territorial size necessarily impedes acceptance into the family of nations. The more territorial fragmentation occurs in the world society, the larger will be the number of small and microstates—and the greater will be the international needs and problems they engender.

Policy Issues

Unless the community of nations permits itself to continue to grow unrestrained and is unconcerned about fragmentation and expansion, a number of basic questions must find prompt answers. The position of most states is already compromised by their failure to prescribe a formula for the nature of the global society or a line of demarcation for modern statehood and their reluctance to question a territory's ability to sustain its political individuality and contribute usefully to the development and progress of the international community.

The forces impelling fragmentation today—decolonization, the principle of self-determination, action (often interventionist) for self-government and statehood, and even the granting of independence by the colonial or parent country—seem insufficient to justify participation by microstates as equals in the affairs of the society of nations. The rights and responsibilities of nation-states in relation to those of the larger international community appear to be constrained by a pervading attitude that the global society must continue to be fragmented for the sake of democratization.

To what extent should emergent diminutive states be permitted to become minimal participants or even dependents of the world

---

[48] As noted, this approximates the size of Colorado. Three of these twenty-one countries have less than 1 million people, and the other eighteen have populations between 1 and 5 million. Of the latter, the largest in territorial size exceed half a million square miles (Mali and Mongolia) and five others exceed 400,000 square miles.

[49] The exceptions are El Salvador, Luxembourg, and Vatican City.

23

community? If such new states are satisfied to be, to some extent, international hermits, quasi independence without equal sovereignty in the world community may be not only tolerable but also preferable to full independence. Perhaps the time has come to consider adding to the current modes of government—dependence, self-government without full international statehood, and independence with sovereign equality—another category: independent self-management of internal and external policy and relations without full status and rights in the councils of the collective global community. This would mean that the family of nations would place some restraints on such states and exclude them from particular diplomatic forums and agencies.

Alternatively, voluntary geographic and functional circumscription may be necessary. Small states may find it advantageous voluntarily to limit their active involvement to their immediate regions, maintaining relations with their neighbors but not participating in the broader international conferences, organizations, and affairs. In varying degrees, selective functional involvement has been practiced by all states, large and small, but the principle is not well served by the inclusion of microstates in hemispheric forums concerned with matters distant to their national interest. Thus the future participation of microstates as equals in such affairs might be restricted by the collective community.

The impetus toward self-determination, independence, and status in the family of nations has accelerated remarkably since World War II, focusing primarily on the noncontiguous colonial holdings of the industrial Western powers. In recent years this movement expanded to include isolated island territories, and it could proceed to encompass separatism and secession of integral state territory. Is it to be assumed that it is too late to restrain this trend, that as a matter of policy change is unnecessary at this time, that lines of demarcation may be drawn later, or that the current international system, in any event, is incapable of retarding the momentum? The primary question is whether current members of the community of nations have an obligation to prescribe realistic terms for nationhood and global participation and to put into effect appropriate policies respecting recognition, accreditation of diplomatic missions, and admission to international conferences and organizations. In short, are there definable limits to universalism of status and participation? If so, what are they, and how may they be applied? Related are matters of national interest and policy and the fundamental issues of national and international capability.

In view of probable future proliferation of statehood, the governments of the United States and other powers need to reassess the fragmentation during recent decades, and attempt to project what the world community may become and what qualities it needs to remain viable. They must determine whether unrestricted splintering and expansion may reach a point of diminishing returns for the family of nations, and what should and can be done about it. The following chapters examine potential proliferation and analyze a number of cardinal aspects of the diplomatic interrelations of states, provide factual data on which responses to such questions may be formulated, and suggest pragmatic alternatives to existing practices.

3
POTENTIAL PROLIFERATION
OF STATES

In view of developments since World War II, estimating the potential expansion of the community of nations becomes a stimulating exercise in supposition. Proliferation of statehood is likely to continue, but on what terms and in what numbers? If projection is limited to unfulfilled promises and already active movements, the territories likely to achieve statehood in the near future would be relatively few, and their independence might be consummated in another generation. More liberal projections may be based on U.N. development of the principles of decolonization, self-determination, and self-government, in which case the list of potential states would be increased substantially. Were consideration to extend to insular possibilities, in particular the many tiny island-territories or "flyspecks of empire," [1] the list of potential states might appear to be almost endless. But it would be longer yet if overlayed by separatism, secession, and fragmentation of the contiguous territory of existing states and by the dismemberment of the former colonies that have become the new colonial powers.

Probable versus Possible Proliferation

Several approaches may be used to identify probable candidates for statehood. For example, speculation could be restricted to the ninety territories on the agenda of the United Nations in recent years for consideration as non-self-governing territories. Though nearly half of these have gained their independence, the remaining territories are

---

[1] An expression used by Robert G. Kaiser in the *Washington Post*, August 15, 1965.

still extensive and prime candidates.[2] An alternative compilation restricted to entities under 300,000 in population, published in 1968 in a Carnegie Endowment study, identifies some sixty-five territories, of which one-fourth have become independent or have been annexed to other states.[3] In 1969, the Department of State also contemplated the creation within a few years of an additional fifty states, each with a population of less than 100,000.[4]

While these lists differ in detail as to the territories included, liberally construed they imply the probable addition of at least 50 states to the family of nations, increasing its membership to more than 200. As of January 1976 these potential states included:

Western Hemisphere
  Antigua
  Belize (British Honduras)
  Bermuda
  British Virgin Islands
  Cayman Islands
  Dominica
  Falkland Islands
  French Guiana
  Guadeloupe
  Montserrat
  Netherlands Antilles
  St. Kitts-Nevis-Anguilla
  St. Lucia
  St. Pierre and Miquelon
  St. Vincent
  Turks and Caicos Islands
  Virgin Islands (U.S.)

Europe
  Andorra
  Channel Islands
  Faroe Islands
  Gibraltar
  Isle of Man
  Liechtenstein
  Monaco
  San Marino

Mideast
  Ifni

Sub-Saharan Africa
  Afars and Issas
  Southern Rhodesia
  South West Africa/Namibia
  St. Helena

[2] Seventy-six such territories were identified by the General Assembly in 1960 (see tabulation in "Issues before the Sixteenth General Assembly," *International Conciliation*, no. 534 [September 1961], pp. 96-99). The list was reduced to fifty-five by 1966, but included fourteen territories added since 1960 (see Table 1 in "Issues before the 21st General Assembly," *International Conciliation*, no. 559 [September 1966], pp. 86-87). Of the territories contained in these lists, thirty-five have since become independent states and five have united with, or have been absorbed by, other states—leaving a balance of fifty that might conceivably become independent in the future.

[3] Seventeen of these achieved independence, one joined another state, and two others were absorbed by other states, leaving a balance of forty-five potential microstates. For the list, see Blair, *The Ministate Dilemma*, Table 1, pp. 75-83.

[4] U.S. Department of State, *Gist*, "U.N.: Microstates," no. 2 (October 1969).

Asia and Indian Ocean
  Brunei
  Hong Kong
  Macao
  Portuguese Timor *
  Seychelles **

Oceania
  American Samoa
  Cocos (Keeling) Islands
  Cook Islands
  French Polynesia
  Gilbert and Ellice Islands

Guam
Micronesia
New Caledonia
New Hebrides
Nieue
Norfolk Island
Pitcairn Island
Solomon Islands
Tokelau Islands
Wallis and Futuna

Arctic
  Greenland

* Absorbed by Indonesia.
** Now independent.

Although all of these appeared in the U.N. or Carnegie Endowment lists, or both, the inclusion of some may be questioned, such as Greenland, Hong Kong, Macao, and Portuguese Timor. In 1953 Greenland was constitutionally incorporated as an integral part of the Danish realm. Portuguese Timor has been annexed by Indonesia as noted earlier, but is hypothetically revivable as a candidate for independence. It may be contended that Hong Kong and Macao will eventually be reannexed by China. However, these are conjectures and one can only predict with confidence that the candidates for statehood will change over time. Certain territories appearing on the list will need to be deleted, some may be amalgamated, others may be further divided, and still others will have to be added. The Seychelles and Transkei (a section of South Africa) gained independence in 1976, and Afars and Issas, Namibia, and Southern Rhodesia are likely to follow in the next few years. Additional possibilities for the near future include Belize, French Guiana, the Gilbert and Ellice (Tuvalu) Islands, Guadeloupe, and the Netherlands Antilles. While the Mariana Islands are being converted into an American commonwealth, the future of the Caroline and Marshall islands, in the United States Pacific Trust Territory (Micronesia), is likely to be debated. In 1976 the United Nations brought pressure on the United States to prepare the Virgin Islands for independence, and the status of Puerto Rico is frequently the focus of U.N. deliberation.

If a list of potential states were compiled based on possibilities rather than probabilities, it would be far more extensive and would entail many more uncertainties. For example, the compilation provided in Appendix B, employing liberal inclusion for purposes of theoretical analysis, lists 150 candidate territories. Statistics concerning them are summarized in Table 3.

A large majority of the candidates tabulated here—more than two-thirds—are colonial dependencies.[5] A few former dependent territories, ceded by the parent to other countries, are included because they conceivably may revert to seeking independence.[6] Approximately twenty others are regarded by the metropolitan countries to be integral parts of their domain but, because of their noncontiguous or insular status, may be viewed as potentially separable for statehood.[7] Other candidates include the Chinese peripheral provinces,[8] quasi-independent territories (the four traditional European principalities[9] and Southern Rhodesia), and former independent countries that have been either forcibly absorbed by other states[10] or peacefully annexed by, or united with, another country.[11] The remainder consists of entities whose status is unsettled[12] or disputed.[13]

This list could be extended considerably by including additional types of territories. For example, certain islands or island-groups might be separated from archipelagoes or other insular administration. To name only a few, this could involve the separation of paired islands, including components of existing states such as Trinidad/Tobago and São Tomé/Príncipe, or the separation of Fernando Po from Rio Muni (which togther constitute Equatorial Guinea), or such combinations as the British Channel Islands (Guernsey and Jersey), the Andaman

---

[5] This designation of colonial status is used in the generic rather than in any precise technical or constitutional sense—largely noncontiguous territories, irrespective of the degree of incorporation into the political, governmental, social, and economic systems of the metropolitan countries.

[6] Ifni, ceded by Spain to Morocco in 1969; West Irian, ceded by the Netherlands to Indonesia via temporary U.N. administration in the 1960s; and the Spanish Sahara, ceded by Spain to Morocco and Mauritania in 1975.

[7] The French, Greek, and Italian islands in the Mediterranean (Corsica, Crete, Majorca and Minorca, Sardinia, and others), the Aleutians, the Canadian arctic islands, and Greenland.

[8] Inner Mongolia, Manchuria, Sinkiang/Turkestan, and Tibet. Of course these are long-range and hypothetical rather than currently likely possibilities for independence, but Tibet, for example, has been restive.

[9] Andorra, Liechtenstein, Monaco, and San Marino.

[10] Estonia, Latvia, and Lithuania, annexed by the Soviet Union, and Goa, taken over by India in 1961.

[11] Hawaii (U.S.), Newfoundland (Canada), Sikkim (India), and Zanzibar (which combined with Tanganyika to establish Tanzania in 1964).

[12] Antarctica, for example.

[13] Kashmir (India and Pakistan), the Panama Canal Zone (Panama and the United States), and Tierra del Fuego (Argentina and Chile).

and Nicobar Islands (India), Canton and Enderbury (United Kingdom/ United States), and Wallis and Futuna (France). Larger colonial insular groupings also may be dismembered, including the Canadian Northwest Territories islands,[14] the Gilbert and Ellice Islands, the Netherlands Antilles,[15] the Solomons, and the Virgin Islands, or even established island-states—Indonesia, Japan, New Zealand, the Philippines, and the United Kingdom [16]—and island-continental combinations like Malaysia.[17]

Other hypothetical secessionist possibilities involve continental territories such as the Basque provinces of Spain, Bessarabia, Bohemia, Kurdistan, Quebec, the Saar, Scotland, Serbia, and certain Soviet republics, as well as noncontiguous integral territories represented by Alaska, Cabinda (Angola), European Turkey, Hainan (China), Gotland (Sweden), Northern Ireland, Vancouver Island (Canada), and Zealand (Denmark). Theoretically, the list of such secessionist potentialities may be regarded as virtually boundless and even though serious projection concerning the entire group may seem like mental gymnastics, reports concerning separatist factions and movements in a good many of them have appeared in the press in recent years. Some of the territories that recently gained independence would scarcely have been considered likely prospects for statehood a few years ago.

Were the independence movement to penetrate this deeply, especially if the principle of self-determination should be applied to separatist and secessionist movements to the extent that it has been employed by the United Nations against pre-Charter colonialism, the proliferation and realignment of the community of nations would appear to be endless. Although the post-World War II independence momentum has not fully abated, it does not seem likely that the most extravagant conception of fragmentation and independence will materialize. Nevertheless, if history is any guide to the future, while some territories will amalgamate, many others are yet to separate and emerge into statehood and international status.

---

[14] A dozen of these are listed in Appendix B, to which might be added Borden, King William, Prince Patrick, and other smaller islands.

[15] Aruba, Bonaire, Curaçao, Saba, St. Eustatius, and part of St. Martin.

[16] The Philippine Republic consists of over 7,000 islands, and Indonesia, territorially the world's largest archipelago, comprises about 3,000 islands. Even if potential fragmentation is restricted to the main islands, these two groups could be broken up into nearly two dozen separate island-states.

[17] Malaysia consists of the Malay peninsula and Sabah and Sarawak in the northern part of the island of Borneo.

Table 3

POTENTIAL EXPANSION OF COMMUNITY OF NATIONS

Geographic Area	Potential nations (number)	Insular status		Expansion Possibility														
		Islands	Conti-nental	Population category							Dependency							
				0^a	A	B	C	D	E	F	Semi-indep.	Disputed	Australia	France	U.K.	U.S.	U.S.S.R.	Others
Western Hemisphere	31	28	3	2	21	4	3	1						5	13	6		7
Europe	23	14	9		12	3	2	6			4			1	3		3	12
Mideast and North Africa	4	2	2		1	2	1											4
Sub-Saharan Africa	6	3	3		3		2	1						1	2			2
Asia and Indian Ocean	23	16	7	2	4	5	5	5	1	1	1	3		1	3		2	14
Oceania	46	46	0	8	33	3	2					1	10	7	6	14		8
Arctic	9	9	0	6	3												5	4
Antarctic	8	7	1	7	1							1		2	3			2
Total	150	125	25	25	78	17	14	14	1	1	5	5	10	17	30	20	10	53

Community of Nations after Expansion

Geographic Area	All nations			Island nations			Population category										
	1975	New	Total	1975	New	Total	0 [a]	A	B	C	D	E	F	G	H	I	J
Western Hemisphere	29	31	60	8	28	36	2	22	6	6	12	9	1	1	1		1
Europe	32	23	55	5	14	19		13	4	5	11	14	4	3	1		1
Mideast and North Africa	21	4	25	—	2	2		1	5	2	7	7	3				
Sub-Saharan Africa	42	6	48	5	3	8	2	4	3	9	20	10	1	1			
Asia and Indian Ocean	24	23	47	6	16	22	2	4	6	5	9	10	5	2		2	2
Oceania	7	46	53	6	46	52	8	35	4	3	2	1					
Arctic	—	9	9	—	9	9	6	3									
Antarctic	—	8	8	—	7	7	7	1									
Total	155	150	305	30	125	155	25	83	28	30	61	51	14	6	1	2	4

a Wholly or largely uninhabited.

Source: Table 1, Table 2, and Appendix B.

33

Results of Possible Proliferation

If the more probable candidates—the non-self-governing entities considered by the United Nations, those listed in the Carnegie Endowment study of microstates, or those included in the Department of State projection of submicrostates—were to gain individual statehood, the world community would grow by another third and exceed 200 members. In view of recent experience this may not be entirely visionary.

Were all the territories listed in Appendix B to gain independence, the society of nations would exceed 300 members. The most extensive increases would occur in the Western Hemisphere (largely the Caribbean area) and Oceania, which would jointly account for half of the new states. Europe (especially the Mediterranean) and Asia (including the Indian Ocean) would also contribute substantially. On the other hand, reversing the trend of the 1960s and early 1970s, sub-Saharan Africa would experience little additional growth. As a consequence, the geographic composition of the world would change to the following regional priorities: the Western Hemisphere (60 states), Europe (55), Oceania (53), sub-Saharan Africa (48), Asia and the Indian Ocean (47), the Mideast and North Africa (25), and the polar regions (17), as indicated in Table 1. In this sequence Africa, which now constitutes the largest quantitative component, would be exceeded by three other geographic regions; these three regions—the Western Hemisphere, Europe, and Oceania—would account for 55 percent of the expanded family of nations.

From World War II to 1976, as is well known, the preponderant majority of the new states were previously British, French, Portuguese, and Belgian territories.[18] This situation would change if the 150 potential states became independent, as indicated in Table 3. The United Kingdom and France would still rank high in the list of administering governments but their relative contribution would decline,[19] although together with Australia, the Soviet Union, and the United States, they would account for nearly 60 percent of the total

---

[18] Nearly 85 percent of the newly independent territories previously belonged to these four powers: United Kingdom—45 percent, France—29 percent, Portugal—6 percent, and Belgium—4 percent. Other former colonial powers—Australia, Denmark, the Netherlands, New Zealand, Spain, and the United States—accounted for 8 percent, and most of the remaining dependent territories were under joint administration, though a few were quasi-independent or broke off from other states.

[19] The United Kingdom accounts for 20 percent and France for 11 percent.

number of new states.[20] Ten other countries—Canada, China, Greece, India, Italy, Japan, New Zealand, Norway, Portugal, and Spain—would contribute from three to five new states apiece. As indicated in Appendix B, other countries could also be involved, including Argentina, Chile, Denmark, Ecuador, Morocco, Norway, Tanzania, Venezuela, and the Yemen. This shift from the handful of traditional European colonial powers to a dispersed agglomeration of disparate states reflects a material change in the essence of movement to independence. The distribution would be even more diversified if potential separatist and secessionist territories were included.

More important to future international politics and foreign policy development, the addition of these 150 territories would alter considerably the ratio of smaller and insular states. Table 3 indicates that just 2 of these potential countries exceed 5 million in population (Inner Mongolia and Manchuria) and that only 28 more surpass 300,000.[21] These 30 represent only 20 percent of the potential increase. The remaining 120 are microstates, and of these 1 of every 5 is now uninhabited and 78, having populations below 100,000, are submicrostates. If all became independent, the composition of the family of nations would then consist of 136 microstates (44.6 percent), 91 small (29.8 percent), 65 medium-sized (21.3 percent), and 13 large states (04.3 percent). Thus, approximately three-fourths of the members of the community of nations would have populations of less than 5 million, and more than four of every ten would be microstates. Inasmuch as five-sixths of the territories listed in Appendix B constitute islands and archipelagoes,[22] more than half of the more than 300 members of the future society of nations would be insular in nature.[23] That is, the larger states on the great continental landmasses would be outnumbered by galaxies of small island-states.

Results of More Limited Proliferation

Viewing future expansion and the consequent composition of the family of nations more conservatively, and perhaps more realistically,

---

[20] United States—13 percent, Australia—7 percent, and the Soviet Union—7 percent.

[21] Fourteen of these are currently under 1 million, which means that only about 10 percent of the new states exceed this figure. Comment regarding the likelihood of independence for the Chinese peripheral provinces was mentioned earlier.

[22] One hundred twenty-five of the 150 are insular. See Appendix B and Table 3.

[23] See Table 3.

one would presume certain types of territories listed in Appendix B would appear unlikely to gain independence and may be discounted. These embrace such categories as the integral components of existing states, the long-held Chinese peripheral provinces, most polar and other uninhabited lands, and a number of individual territories like the Panama Canal Zone and the Saar. On this basis, some fifty territories could be deleted, reducing the potential membership of the family of nations to approximately 250 states. This still amounts to quadrupling the world community since World War II. Nearly half of the reduction according to this formula involves European and Oceanian territories, and the polar regions might virtually disappear from the list, whereas the Mideast and sub-Saharan African quotas continue unaltered. The pattern of areal priorities would change, and, though sub-Saharan Africa could emerge with the second largest number of states, the Western Hemisphere, Europe, and Oceania could continue to represent over half of the family of nations. Although the quantity of island states would be reduced from 51 to 44 percent, they would continue to constitute an influential segment of the family of nations.

Most important for this analysis, perhaps, is the finding that the changes in relative population ratios in a 250-member community of nations would reduce the small states (under 5 million) only from about 75 percent to 70 percent. Nearly 100 (38 percent of the total) would be microstates, of which 7 of every 10 would be submicrostates. Should this occur—or even be approached—international affairs would be seriously affected, because more than one of every four members of the community of nations would be under 100,000 in population, and, at least theoretically, a tyranny of the majority of states in a global forum could represent only a small fraction of the world's population.

In other words, Nauru and Grenada, sovereign states today, could be followed by not only Andorra, Monaco, San Marino, and a few of the more populous islands like Hong Kong (3.9 million) and Puerto Rico (2.7 million) but also by a host of sparsely settled insular territories such as the Bonin, Cocos (Keeling), Falkland, Midway, Nieue, St. Helena, St. Pierre and Miquelon, Tokelau, Turks and Caicos, and Wake islands—all of which currently are smaller than Nauru in population and have been on the U.N. self-determination lists.[24] It also means that India, Japan, and the United Kingdom would be

[24] Each of these is under 6,000 in population. Others of similar size (under 7,000) but not on the U.N. list include Anguilla, Christmas, Corn, Johnston atoll, Kurile, Marquesas, Norfolk, and Volcano islands.

balanced, as voting equals, by Ascension, Fanning, and Washington islands—each with under 500 people, and that such major powers as China, the Soviet Union, and the United States could be offset by tiny Pitcairn, South Georgia, and Swain's islands, each of which has less than 100 inhabitants.

Thus, in the future, a large number of sparsely populated countries may be in a position to exercise disproportionate influence on international problems, priorities, and procedures. Almost all small states are members of the Third World—in which they constitute a two-thirds majority—and they generally stand together on certain types of issues in multilateral forums. Their role will be further enlarged by increasing the number of microstates. This could result in increased diplomatic, economic, political, and social demands upon other countries and the global society by groups of such states, and in new problems of linking responsibility to a capacity to contribute to both action and funding. All other considerations aside, these relationships are bound to bear directly upon voice and voting power in international decision making, particularly in connection with the progression of decolonization and territorial fragmentation.

Policy Issues

To contend that such a proliferation of diminutive states in the world community is speculative and not likely to materialize in practice scarcely gainsays the facts that diminutive Nauru did become independent in 1968, that the population of Vatican City is under 1,000, that the independence of a substantial number of the small territories listed in Appendix B has been, and continues to be, considered by the United Nations, and that the press has been replete with reports on independence movements and actions in some of these and in others as well. Pitcairn Island, for example, appears on both the U.N. and Carnegie Endowment lists, and if it may envision statehood,[25] then why not Montserrat, Socotra, Norfolk Island, Key West,

[25] See Arthur Hoppe's brief satire titled "Pitcairn Island: The Ideal State," in which he proclaims that the Pacific island has "ideal requisites for nationhood": a rich history, pleasant climate, a few square miles "of sacred soil to defend," a single thriving industry which produces something always in demand (postage stamps), and "a strategic position in world affairs—it being 5,000 miles from anywhere." The only objection to statehood, he spoofingly discerns, is its limited population. Published in the *San Francisco Chronicle* and republishhed in *War/Peace Report*, vol. 7 (April 1967), p. 6.

or even a future man-made coral pimple in the Pacific? [26] Moreover, if the Cayman, Cocos (Keeling), Nieue, and Tokelau islands are proper candidates for consideration for self-government and independence—as they have been in the United Nations—what about the many other territories which, though they may not be on any U.N. agenda, have recently been reported in the press to be restive? These include such insular territories as Corsica (France), Northern Ireland (United Kingdom), and the Moluccas (Indonesia), and such continental territories as the Basque provinces of Spain, Brittany (France), southern Sudan, the Moslem sections of the Philippines, and southern India (Tamil Nadu).

Nor can it be ignored that the Union of Expelled Sudeten Germans acquired 100,000 signatures in support of a petition demanding the same rights and status in the United Nations as that accorded the Palestine Liberation Organization. Or that a nation of 15,000 Eskimos filed a formal claim with the Canadian government to obtain special rights to some 750,000 square miles of landed territory and 800,000 square miles of ocean space and the formation of a separate political jurisdiction for them. Or that a group of Hawaiians adopted a declaration of independence, proclaimed their right to deal with the United States as a sovereign nation, and demanded $1 billion and 2.5 million acres of land. Yet, all of these have occurred in recent years.

---

[26] In 1972 the press reported plans of the Ocean Life Research Foundation to construct two small coral islands on the Minerva Reefs (coral formations) lying between Fiji and Tonga. The reefs are exposed only at ebb tide, so the plan was to move coral and sand to raise the level to ten feet above high tide, and to proclaim the new territory the Republic of Minerva. The foundation allegedly planted a specially fabricated national flag and requested recognition by other states. See *Washington Post*, February 16, 1972.

Three years later it was reported that Jacques Cousteau, well-known undersea explorer and leader of Eurocean, a twenty-three-member European consortium, was designing two man-made islands, one to be located in the North Sea between the Netherlands and Great Britain as a 2.5-acre industrial site, and the other as a floating resort island off the coast of Monaco to accommodate 10,000 people. Other projected man-made islands include a recreation territory planned for Long Island Sound and an "Atlantis in the Pacific"—a twenty-five-acre floating platform off the shores of Honolulu to accommodate 40,000 visitors and a servicing staff of several hundred people. See *Parade*, March 16, 1975, p. 16. Another such futuristic venture is the "Aquapolis," a $43 million three-story, self-propelled modular creation, afloat off the island of Okinawa; see the *Washington Star*, September 30, 1976.

Even more fanciful, in 1976 a number of scientists at the Ames Research Center reportedly proposed placing a medium-sized city in an earthlike habitat out in space some 240,000 miles from the earth, pioneering new ventures in "space colonies"—as an innovation of the new world of the twenty-first century. See *Washington Star*, June 18, 1976.

New states, apparently regardless of population size, are qualified for participation in international affairs, may establish regularized diplomatic relations and engage in international conferences and treaty making, and cast votes in international organizations. Because of their sovereign equality with other states, their participation is certain to alter the nature and functioning of the community of nations. The community accordingly must consider the lengths to which it will go to accommodate so many diminutive entities, facilitate their international involvement, ease their global community burdens, and stretch its standards concerning sovereign equality.

To illustrate the strange interrelations that could ensue if the family of nations added 150 more members (as in one hypothesis described above), it may be noted that the People's Republic of China, the most populous state, would be more than four times as large as all of the 227 existing and projected small states (Categories A to D) combined, which would amount to only 188.7 million. Each of the next three most populous countries (India, the Soviet Union, and the United States) would also exceed the aggregate population of these small entities. Yet the small states would jointly compose three-fourths of this enlarged community of nations. No fewer than sixty-seven of the medium-sized and larger states (for example, Austria, Chile, Iraq, or Uganda) would exceed the combined population of the 136 existing and projected microstates. A single medium-sized country like Belgium is four times the size, in population, of the sixteen current microstates combined—or of all the forty-six future states in Oceania.

The United States is more populous than the projected 227 small states combined. It is nearly 50 percent more populous than all of the seventy-nine existing small states (under 5 million) and four times as populous as all 148 projected small states combined. Inasmuch as the current average microstate population is somewhat less than 150,000, the United States alone would balance some 1,350 of them. Given the legal equality of sovereign members of the society of nations, the United States suffers such gross inequalities in per capita representation as being equivalent to 0.06 percent of the Maldives or 0.003 percent of Nauru, and would constitute the ridiculous equivalent of 0.00004 percent of Pitcairn or Swain's Island.

It seems plain from the foregoing that the policy issues raised center upon, not *whether*, *why*, or *when*, but *how* to manage current and prospective growth of the global community. Realistic distinctions must be drawn and applied to a country's diminutiveness as it affects both statehood and participation in transnational and world relations. Policy analysis also needs to be focused on the consequences of liberalized application of the principle of self-determination, and on alternative options for coping with the transformed character of the international community that will result if fragmentation and proliferation of nation-states continue.

4

DIPLOMATIC RELATIONS

Diplomacy is the political process whereby states establish and nurture official interrelations, direct and indirect, to pursue their respective goals, interests, and substantive and procedural policies in the international environment.[1] It would seem logical that all states, large and small, old and new, would employ it maximally in dealing with other members of the global community. The assumption is generally valid that states engage actively in the diplomatic relations of the world. They vary substantially, however, in the methods, the procedures, and the forums they utilize. Among the leading and more obvious aspects of such interrelations are direct bilateral diplomatic representation, treaty and agreement making, and participation in international conferences and in the activities of international organizations.

States differ considerably in the reasons for, and the degree of intensity of, their engagement in these diplomatic processes. Some tend to become universally involved, while others prefer or are obliged to be more selective. Some are comprehensive in their interests and become dedicated joiners, whereas others circumscribe their concerns and involvement. Certain states assume the guise of consummate participants largely out of a sense of responsibility to the international community as well as to themselves, many are attracted more by the benefits they expect to achieve, and others are impelled by the appeal and importance of the international political process and their positions within it, and they find national gratification if not pragmatic political advantage in "playing the game."

---

[1] Elmer Plischke, "The Optimum Scope of Instruction in Diplomacy," *Instruction in Diplomacy: The Liberal Arts Approach*, ed. Smith Simpson (Philadelphia: American Academy of Political and Social Science, 1972), pp. 1-25, especially p. 20.

Traditional Bilateral Diplomatic Representation

The impression that, once a state becomes a member of the community of nations, it establishes and maintains regularized diplomatic representation bilaterally with all other states is far from the truth. While the mutual exchange of resident diplomatic missions is generally regarded as normal international procedure, the amount of nonrepresentation is surprising. The earlier practice of establishing diplomatic relations upon recognition, or in effect basing them on political acceptability, has diminished as a major reason for the absence of representational interchange. Although lack of recognition is still determining in certain circumstances, more important factors contributing to nonrepresentation include the mounting demands for personnel and financial and communications resources to maintain relations with an ever-increasing congeries of dissimilar states throughout the world. This is especially true among the growing number of small states, many of which are hopelessly ill-equipped to cope with such demands. The consequence is a vexatious problem for a burgeoning number of states which, if they are to function effectively in the enlarged global society, need to devise alternatives to the traditional bilateral representational process.

In 1975 the 155 members of the international community maintained nearly 6,400 regular resident diplomatic missions at each other's capitals (see Appendix A for statistics on the diplomatic representation of individual countries). As might be expected, only the older, larger and more politically active states maintain wholesale direct diplomatic representation to other countries. At present no government commissions resident emissaries to all others, and only sixteen (10 percent) accredit regularized missions to more than 100 countries,[2] as shown in Table 4. Austria, Belgium, the Netherlands, the United Kingdom, and the United States commission the largest number of diplomatic missions.[3]

---

[2] Austria, Belgium, Canada, Denmark, France, the Federal Republic of Germany, India, Italy, the Netherlands, Norway, Romania, Sweden, Switzerland, the United Kingdom, the U.S.S.R., and the United States. Note that all of these, except India, antedate World War II, and all of them, except India and the United States, are European powers. Nine countries maintain ninety to ninety-nine diplomatic missions: Bulgaria, the People's Republic of China, Finland, Hungary, Japan, Pakistan, Poland, Spain, and Yugoslavia.

[3] In 1975, the figures were: Austria (140), the Netherlands (136), the United Kingdom (134), Belgium (132), and the United States (131). Austria, the Netherlands, and the United States, however, resorted to some simultaneous multiple representation. As of January 1977 the United States increased its diplomatic community to 138, largely by establishing representation in additional new countries.

Only thirty-four states maintain relations with seventy or more members of the global community, leaving almost four out of every five national governments unrepresented by resident missions in more than half of the other countries. As indicated in Table 4, one of the thirty-four states with high diplomatic representation is a microstate (Vatican City [4]) and three others are numbered among the small countries with populations under 5 million (Denmark, Finland, and Norway). Of the twenty-five states maintaining the highest quotas of diplomatic missions (to more than ninety countries), all but six are European powers,[5] and all but three (India, Pakistan, and the People's Republic of China) antedate World War II.

The average number of diplomatic missions per state in 1975 was forty-three,[6] but nearly three of five countries rank below this average. Of these, about 30 percent accredit emissaries to between twenty-one and forty other countries and, surprisingly, about 40 percent of the nations send emissaries to fewer than twenty other states. These vary from Bolivia (with 19 missions), Zambia (17), and Luxembourg (16), to Guyana (10), Gambia (6), and Bhutan (2).[7] Moreover, a substantial number of states (32) maintain relations only with the United States or the United Kingdom, or both, and eleven accredit no missions at all (see lower part of Table 4).[8]

Evidencing the paucity of their diplomatic representation, nearly 90 percent of the smaller countries that have less than 1 million popu-

---

[4] The Vatican maintains diplomatic relations with seventy-seven governments, fairly well distributed throughout the world. Monaco and San Marino are included, but not the United States. Vatican missions are not restricted to Catholic countries. For a general but comprehensive account of the diplomacy of the Holy See, see Robert A. Graham, *Vatican Diplomacy* (Princeton: Princeton University Press, 1959), with an extensive bibliography. For a record of U.S. representation to Vatican City, see Plischke, *United States Diplomats and Their Missions*, Table A-1, p. 154; Table A-2, p. 158; Table A-5, pp. 174-175; and Table A-14, p. 197.

[5] The exceptions are the United States, Canada, the People's Republic of China, India, Japan, and Pakistan.

[6] This computation excludes the seven new states that gained independence in 1975: Angola, Cape Verde Islands, Comoro Islands, Mozambique, Papua New Guinea, Surinam, and São Tomé and Príncipe. If the computation is limited to the 112 states for which detailed information was available, the average would be approximately 57.

[7] Bhutan sends missions only to two of its immediate neighbors—India and Bangladesh.

[8] Aside from the newer states that joined the family of nations in 1974 and 1975, which have not had time to do much about diplomatic representation, these include the Soviet republics (Byelorussia and the Ukraine, which send no resident missions), Nauru (whose diplomacy is handled by Australia), Western Samoa, and the Yemen (Aden).

Table 4

NUMBER OF DIPLOMATIC MISSIONS OF THE NATIONS OF THE WORLD

Number of Missions	Nations with this Number	Population Category a										Geographic Area						New Nations (since 1940)			
		A	B	C	D	E	F	G	H	I	J	W. Hemi-sphere	Europe	Mideast	Africa b	Asia	Oceania	Micro	Small	Others	Total
Over 101	16				2	7	1	3			3	2	13			1				1	1
91–100	9					3	2	1	1	1	1		6			3				2	2
81–90	3				2	1						1	1			1				1	1
71–80	6	1		1		1	2	1				2	2	1		1				2	2
61–70	7				1	5	1					1	1	2	1	1	1		1	2	3
51–60	11				3	8						3	1	2	2	3				6	6
41–50	15		1	2	3	5	2	1		1		2	3	5	1	3	1	1	3	4	8
31–40	15				8	6	1					4		3	2	6			4	6	10
21–30	15				7	6	2					6	1	2	4	2			2	3	5
11–20	12			2	6	3	1					3	2	1	5	1			6	1	7
1–10	3			2		1						1			1	1			2	1	3
With U.S./U.K. c	32	2	7	8	14	1						3		4	21	1	3	10	21	1	32
None/not known d	11	2	3	1	1	3	1					1	2e	1	5		2	4	3	4	11f
Total	155	5	11	16	47	50	13	6	1	2	4	29	32	21	42	24	7	15	42	34	91

44

a Micro, A-B; Small, C-D; Medium, E-F; Large, G-J.

b Sub-Saharan Africa.

c Indicates nations maintaining diplomatic missions only to United States and/or United Kingdom; all post-1940.

d Indicates nations maintaining no diplomatic missions, or information not available; includes the most recent states.

e Byelorussia and the Ukraine.

f Eleven plus Byelorussia and the Ukraine.

Source: Based on Appendix A.

lation (categories A to C) accredit diplomatic emissaries to fewer than twenty foreign capitals.[9] Two-thirds of the states with such low diplomatic representation have emerged since World War II, and half are located in sub-Saharan Africa. Except for Vatican City and Iceland, the microstates (population categories A and B) maintain virtually no regularized diplomatic representation abroad,[10] averaging less than one mission per microstate. This excessive degree of noninvolvement in the normal diplomatic process reflects either their unwillingness or their inability to sustain a representational apparatus, and, if the latter, alternatives need to be devised to accommodate their requirements, especially as more small states are permitted to emerge as members of the international community.

Of the forty-eight post-World War II states for which specific information is available, fifteen have more than fifty diplomatic missions abroad, twenty-three maintain from twenty-one to fifty missions, and ten have twenty or fewer missions. In the case of forty-three additional states, however, either insufficient information is available or they have established little or no diplomatic representation. Of these, nearly three-fourths have become independent since 1960. Therefore, more than half of the states that have joined the family of nations since World War II have little or no direct diplomatic representation to other countries. While population size evidently influences the extent of a newer state's diplomatic activity and its involvement in bilateral representational exchanges, recency of independence also becomes a critical factor, most often in connection with diminutiveness.

Alternative Methods of Diplomatic Representation

To understand the problem of nonrepresentation of many of the smaller states, several factors must be taken into account. As new states emerge, they may take several years to develop their diplomatic representational capacities and systems. Some make the transition fairly rapidly (such as Bangladesh, the Republic of Korea, India, Israel, Pakistan, and Tanzania—all of which accredit missions to more than

[9] The four exceptions that exceed twenty missions are Iceland, Kuwait, Malta, and Vatican City.

[10] Only five of sixteen, for example, accredit missions to the United States, namely, the Bahamas, Barbados, Iceland, Qatar, and the United Arab Emirates; states like Bahrain, Equatorial Guinea, the Maldives, and Tongo do not, but the Vatican would in all probability send a mission to Washington if the United States agreed to regularize diplomatic exchange.

sixty governments), but many other post-World War II states have moved more slowly.[11] Often smaller countries begin by establishing diplomatic representation on a limited, selective basis, initially to major world powers, immediate and regional neighbors, countries in which key international organizations have their headquarters, and important trade and security partners; they then expand their diplomatic communities gradually as warranted by their resources and needs.[12] Certain older small states, mostly in the Western Hemisphere, also continue to restrict their diplomatic exchange.[13]

Selectivity, however natural and necessary, seems to have more cogency for explaining the nature of the nonrepresentation problem than for resolving it. As a consequence, alternative methods of diplomatic representation have been developed to bridge the gulf between the desire of nations to maintain adequate bilateral relations and their ability to do so. As illustrated in Figure 1, the alternatives include unilateral, simultaneous multiple, third-country, and joint representation, as well as the conduct of multiple bilateral diplomacy at neutral sites, including the headquarters of important international organizations. Choice of alternatives varies from state to state, and the cooperation of many governments is essential to make them function effectively.

Unilateral Representation. Although it is normal practice for states to exchange diplomatic emissaries,[14] smaller states, to a considerable

---

[11] At least fourteen in existence for more than ten years, mostly sub-Saharan African countries, still have almost no diplomatic representation abroad.

[12] In fifteen years, for example, Cyprus, a post-World War II (1960) small state (category C population), established eleven missions: Belgium, Egypt, France, the Federal Republic of Germany, Greece, Kenya, the Soviet Union, Turkey, the United Kingdom, the United States, and Yugoslavia—all European and Mideast powers except the United States and Kenya. See Cyprus, Ministry of Foreign Affairs, *List of the Diplomatic Corps in Cyprus*, April 1975, pp. 122-126. Similarly, the Ivory Coast and Somalia, also created in 1960, accredit missions to the United States, major European powers, and neighboring African states (although Somalia also sends resident envoys to several nearby Mideast governments). Trinidad and Tobago (1962) maintains missions in Ethiopia, India, Switzerland, and the United Kingdom, in addition to those appointed to major and nearby Western Hemisphere powers.

[13] By way of illustration, Bolivia, a member of the diplomatic community since the mid-nineteenth century, continues selective diplomatic representation, sending emissaries to eight European states, Israel, and ten Western Hemisphere countries, including the United States. Ethiopia sends ten missions to Europe, three to major Asian powers, two to the Western Hemisphere (the United States and Mexico), and twelve to African and Mideast countries.

[14] Article 2 of the 1961 Vienna Convention on Diplomatic Relations provides: "The establishment of diplomatic relations between States, and of permanent

Figure 1
METHODS OF DIPLOMATIC REPRESENTATION

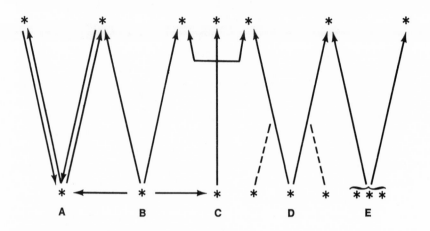

A Bilateral representation (bidirectional relations)
B Unilateral representation (one-way relations)
C Simultaneous multiple representation (single emissary to more than one country)
D Third-country representation (one country represented by another)
E Joint representation (two or more states accrediting the same emissary)
F Multiple bilateral representation at third-country capital
G Multiple bilateral representation at headquarters of international organization

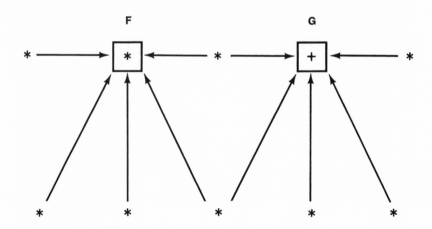

∗ State
+ International organization
← Diplomatic mission

extent, are able to deal diplomatically with other governments through the unilateral representation provided by the other, usually larger, states. One-way representation may be occasional, with an emissary deployed on special or itinerant assignment. Such arrangements offer some mutual representation but more permanent arrangements are better suited to produce more positive results.

While the United States accredited emissaries to 131 countries in 1975, and 125 sent missions to Washington, unilateral relations were maintained by the Department of State through American missions to the governments of 8 countries.[15] The United States enjoys a unique advantage for minimizing unilateral representation because small states that join the United Nations can economically undertake bilateral relations by accrediting a single emissary to represent them both in Washington and New York.

Unilateral diplomatic representation is exemplified by Cyprus, which accredits envoys to only eleven countries, although forty-six send emissaries to Nicosia.[16] Similarly, Sierra Leone sends missions to thirteen countries, but more than fifty commission emissaries to Freetown.[17] The use of unilateral representation has increased with the proliferation of nations since World War II. By this means, small states, having relatively few diplomatic establishments of their own,

---

diplomatic missions, takes place by mutual consent." U.S., Department of State, *United States Treaties and Other International Agreements*, vol. 23, part 3 (1972), p. 3231. Although at times debated, the "right of legation" has existed from ancient times. Independent states possess the unquestionably legal right to send diplomatic agents to represent their interests in other states, and reciprocally to receive such emissaries. A state's sending right is discretionary, and no state can be compelled to accredit diplomatic missions to other capitals, but the state that refuses all diplomatic representation forgoes certain advantages of membership in the world community. For commentary, see Melquaides J. Gamboa, *Elements of Diplomatic and Consular Practice: A Glossary* (Quezon City, Philippines: Central Lawbook Publishing Co., 1966), pp. 175-176; Elmer Plischke, *Conduct of American Diplomacy*, 3rd ed. (Princeton: Van Nostrand, 1967), p. 4; and Graham H. Stuart, *American Diplomatic and Consular Practice*, 2nd ed. (New York: Appleton-Century-Crofts, 1952), pp. 128-129, 132.

[15] Bahrain, Equatorial Guinea, Gambia, Grenada, the Maldives, Nauru, Tonga, and Western Samoa, all of which, except Gambia, are microstates. On the other hand, Uganda sends a mission to Washington even though the American mission to Kampala was closed in 1973. Late in 1975 Papua New Guinea also sent a mission to Washington, although an American mission was not commissioned to Port Moresby until 1976.

[16] Since representation is bilateral with ten governments and Kenya sends no mission to Nicosia but Cyprus maintains one in Nairobi, the total number of states with which Cyprus has bilateral or unilateral representation is forty-seven. See Cyprus, *List of the Diplomatic Corps in Cyprus*.

[17] Sierra Leone, Ministry of Foreign Affairs, *Diplomatic and Consular List*, March 1975.

may actually be in direct relations with substantial segments of the diplomatic community. Nevertheless, under this arrangement they are dependent on the willingness of the larger states to sustain the burden of one-sided representation,[18] and many less endowed states are unable to provide them with this service.

Simultaneous Multiple Representation. Another option for augmenting diplomatic representation is the multiple accreditation of diplomats. Employing this technique, a government commissions a single emissary simultaneously to two or more foreign governments.[19] In such cases the ambassador normally has his residence in one capital and proceeds to the other capital(s) from time to time as required by the pressures of business. Often he has lesser ranking agents, who may be commissioned *chargés d'affaires ad interim*, stationed in those countries where he does not maintain his permanent headquarters.[20] Recognizing the usefulness of multiple representation, Article 5 of the Vienna Convention on Diplomatic Relations of 1961 provides:

> 1. The sending State may, after it has given due notification to the receiving States concerned, accredit a head of mission or assign any member of the diplomatic staff, as the case may be, to more than one State, unless there is express objection by any of the receiving States.
> 2. If the sending State accredits a head of mission to one or more other States it may establish a diplomatic mission headed by a *chargé d'affaires ad interim* in each State where the head of mission has not his permanent seat.[21]

Appendix A indicates the degree to which multiple diplomatic representation is currently employed. While presently thirty-two states (20.6 percent) utilize this practice, in general the newer and smaller states, which would appear to have most to gain, fail to take advantage of it. For example, two-thirds of the states using multiple representation are pre-World War II Western Hemisphere and Euro-

---

[18] Although, presumably, the sending government usually gains some advantage by maintaining the direct diplomatic link, there are circumstances in which the absence of the alternative channel constitutes a serious impediment.

[19] For historical analysis of U.S. practice in employing multiple diplomacy, see Plischke, *U.S. Diplomats and Their Missions*, pp. 32-42 and Table A-7, pp. 180-181.

[20] For brief commentary, see Gamboa, *Elements of Diplomatic and Consular Practice*, p. 363.

[21] *United States Treaties and Other International Agreements*, vol. 23, part 3 (1972), p. 3232.

pean powers,[22] including the United States.[23] Only nine (11.4 percent) of the small states (population categories A to D) avail themselves of this method, of which Iceland is the sole microstate,[24] and all but Laos are European and Western Hemisphere nations.[25]

It is difficult to understand why more of the smaller, newer, and less endowed states do not take advantage of this diplomatic representation technique, because it serves a variety of useful purposes. Some states are employing it minimally—often largely as a temporary measure pending the establishment of regular missions—to deal with emergency situations, or for occasional special negotiations.[26] Others are relying on it as a normalized method of increasing representation on a continuing basis, some with only one or a few combined missions.[27] At the other extreme, the Sudan commissions twenty-six emissaries to represent it to fifty-eight countries, and Iceland assigns nine envoys to forty-one governments, with its ambassador in Washington accredited also to Canada and six Latin American capitals.[28] Similarly, Afghanistan, Austria, Norway, and

---

[22] The remainder consists of three Mideast (Algeria, Iran, and Iraq), two sub-Saharan African (South Africa and the Sudan), and five Asian states (Afghanistan, Republic of Korea, Laos, Nepal, and Thailand). Iceland is the only post-World War II state in the group of twenty-two European and Western Hemisphere states.

[23] In 1975, six U.S. emissaries were accredited simultaneously to nine additional countries as follows: Equatorial Guinea (resident in Cameroon), Fiji, Tonga, and Western Samoa (in New Zealand), the Gambia (in Senegal), Lesotho and Swaziland (in Botswana), the Maldives (in Sri Lanka), and Nauru (in Australia).

[24] Six of the nine—Denmark, El Salvador, Finland, Laos, Norway, and Paraguay—having populations exceeding 2 million are not among the smallest; Luxembourg and Panama have small populations.

[25] Reportedly, in 1975 Laos had resident ambassadors in eleven countries and had envoys accredited to, but not resident in, twenty-four others.

[26] The experience of the United States in this respect during and after World War II is discussed in Plischke, *U.S. Diplomats and Their Missions*, pp. 38-40.

[27] For example, Denmark commissions a single envoy to Thailand and Laos, Colombia sends one to Belgium and Luxembourg, and both Algeria and Guatemala accredit a single emissary to Belgium, the Netherlands, and Luxembourg. Paraguay's mission to West Germany also represents it in Denmark, Norway, and Sweden, and South Africa coalesces its accreditation not only to Belgium and Luxembourg but also to Argentina and Chile, and to Uruguay and Paraguay.

[28] Iceland accredits its missions as follows: Belgium; Denmark (also China, Ireland, and Turkey); France (also Egypt, Ethiopia, Luxembourg, and Yugoslavia); the Federal Republic of Germany (also Greece, Iran, Japan, and Switzerland); Norway (also Czechoslovakia, Israel, Italy, and Poland); Sweden (also Austria and Finland); the Soviet Union (also Bulgaria, East Germany, Hungary, and Romania); the United Kingdom (also the Netherlands, Nigeria, Portugal, and Spain); and the United States (also Argentina, Brazil, Canada, Chile, Cuba, Mexico, and Peru). Each emissary averages nearly five simultaneous assignments. See *The Statesman's Year Book 1975-1976*, p. 1023.

Finland more than double their diplomatic representation abroad by multiple assignments,[29] and the Netherlands and Sweden both augment their diplomatic communities by approximately fifty-five additional states.[30]

Often a single emissary is accredited to a group of regionally related states, such as Central America, parts of Africa,[31] and the Benelux or Scandinavian countries, and some of these arrangements tend to become relatively permanent. At times, however, emissaries on multiple assignment represent their governments to unrelated and noncontiguous states,[32] which suggests less the itinerant nature of the diplomats' assignments than the probability of bilateral diplomacy conducted in a third, or neutral, capital.

Third-Country Representation. Luxembourg, a quasi microstate, solves its diplomatic representation requirements through a combination of techniques. It accredits ten of its own emissaries to seventeen European and Western Hemisphere states.[33] In addition, under an agreement of 1888, the Netherlands represents Luxembourg in fifty-three other countries, expanding the diplomatic community of the small duchy to nearly seventy states. Such third-party guardianship representation is common for states at war or those whose diplomatic relations are severed,[34] and also is used when small states arrange to have other friendly governments manage their foreign relations.

The tiny island-state of Nauru provides an illustration. The United States accredits an ambassador to Nauru, who is however

[29] The figures are as follows: Afghanistan—nineteen emissaries to 46 countries, Austria—fifty-seven to 140 countries, Norway—forty-four to 101 countries, and Finland—forty-three to 92 countries.

[30] The Netherlands—eighty-two envoys to 136 countries, and Sweden—seventy-two to 127 countries.

[31] For example, Austria's five emissaries to Kenya, Nigeria, Senegal, South Africa, and Zaire are also simultaneously accredited to twenty-four other African governments, with one of them serving ten countries. Norway's four envoys to Argentina, Chile, Mexico, and Venezuela also represent Oslo to a dozen other Latin American countries.

[32] For example, Iceland's emissary to Denmark is also commissioned to China and Turkey, its envoy to West Germany also is accredited to Iran and Japan, and its ambassador in London also represents Reykjavik to Nigeria.

[33] Four of Luxembourg's nine emissaries stationed in European capitals also represent it to five additional European countries, and its envoy to Washington is also accredited to Canada and Mexico.

[34] For a comprehensive account on such third-country service by and for the United States, in both peace and war, through World War II, see William M. Franklin, *Protection of Foreign Interests: A Study in Diplomatic and Consular Practice* (Washington, D.C.: Department of State, 1946).

resident at Canberra (Australia), where the island's foreign relations are conducted for it by the Australian government and diplomatic corps. Similarly, the foreign affairs and direct diplomatic representation of the four European principalities are administered by neighboring powers.[35] Many of the smaller states might find it to their advantage to arrange for a friendly nearby country to conduct their official representation to a wider circle of governments, but this requires an exceptional degree of trust to overcome the apprehensions and meet the needs of the deputizing state.

Joint Representation. A related method of resolving limited representational resources is for two governments to accredit a single envoy to represent them both to a third country. Recognizing the possible necessity of resort to this procedure, Article 6 of the Vienna Convention on Diplomatic Relations provides: "Two or more States may accredit the same person as head of mission to another State, unless objection is offered by the receiving State."[36] This practice appears to be most appropriate for friendly, neighboring countries that possess similar cultures and interests, and whose qualified diplomats and funds are restricted.

Perhaps more commonly used in the past,[37] joint representation is rarely employed in contemporary diplomacy.[38] This is somewhat puzzling. If the governments of diminutive countries wish to expand their direct diplomatic relations, and are able to agree upon a particular emissary and to maintain confidence in him, such joint accreditation should help to ameliorate their diplomatic problem. Mutual representation might serve the needs, for example, of such combinations as Fiji and Tonga, Western and American Samoa (were the latter to gain independence), or the European principalities if they achieve sovereign membership in the community of nations. Hypothetically, it also could be employed by such groups of islands as Majorca and Minorca (if each becomes an independent state), the Virgin Islands (if

[35] Andorra by France, Liechtenstein by Switzerland, Monaco by France, and San Marino by Italy. These principalities participate individually in specific aspects of diplomatic relations, as noted later.

[36] *United States Treaties and Other International Agreements*, vol. 23, part 3 (1972), p. 3233.

[37] For example, for a decade prior to 1775 Benjamin Franklin was sent to London to represent the individual and collective interests of Pennsylvania, Massachusetts, New Jersey, and Georgia. See Stuart, *American Diplomatic and Consular Practice*, p. 81.

[38] An apparent rather than a real exception occurs when governments sever diplomatic relations and one of them requests the emissary of a third government to represent it to the country with which relations are broken.

the British and American groups become separate states), or combinations like Aruba-Bonair-Curaçao (Netherlands Antilles) and the Austral-Marquesa-Society-Tuamotu islands (French Polynesia), should they acquire individual statehood.[39] In the event of extensive future creation of insular or other small states, the new governments may find that joint representation increases their diplomatic relations appreciably at relatively low cost. For this reason it may become a common diplomatic practice.

Multiple Bilateral Representation at Neutral Site. Diplomatic representation also may be augmented by the establishment of direct bilateral relations in some neutral capital. Often states that do not have resident diplomatic missions in each other's capitals (whether or not due to lack of formal recognition) deal with each other, on an ad hoc or continuing basis, through their respective emissaries resident in one of the capitals to which they both have accredited missions. For example, before the United States and the People's Republic of China agreed to exchange liaison offices in 1973, they communicated diplomatically for nearly two decades through their ambassadors stationed in Warsaw.

It is not inconceivable that smaller countries could establish networks of interrelations with other states in major diplomatic centers like Washington, Bonn, Brussels, London, New Delhi, Paris, Rome, and Tokyo, or in neutral capitals like Bern and Vienna. These epicenters of universal representation would offer the widest range of official contact and serve as convenient foci of multiple bilateral diplomacy. Although this method of consultation is widely used informally, smaller states might find it to their advantage to institutionalize the process and thereby broaden their diplomatic communities.

Alternatively, small countries may prefer to deal with others bilaterally through resident and special missions accredited to a major international organization, especially if the headquarters is located in or near the capital of a power to which many states send emissaries. The United Nations (especially New York and Geneva), its specialized agencies, the European Economic Community, or Common Market (Brussels), and other regional international organizations, including the Council of Europe (Strasbourg), the League of Arab States (Cairo), the Organization of African Unity (Addis Ababa), and the Organiza-

[39] Other hypothetical combinations include Anguilla-Nevis-St. Kitts (British Leeward Islands), the Andaman-Nicobar Islands (Indian Ocean), and the Gilbert and Ellice Islands (British Pacific dependency), assuming they become separate states.

tion of American States (Washington), are among the most likely diplomatic centers for this purpose. In other cases, special facilities may exist for previously related groupings of states such as the Commonwealth of Nations, which provides machinery to cope with the mutual concerns of nearly three dozen self-governing and independent states and as many colonies and protectorates, and which also constitutes a convenient agency for bilateral discussion.

As small states perceive sufficient need and develop the requisite resources for doing so, they are likely to expand their bilateral exchange of traditional diplomatic missions. However, most microstates, especially the diminutive, isolated islands, may encounter insurmountable difficulty in broadening their diplomatic horizons. Lacking motivation, adequate manpower, or financial resources, the smaller states may be induced or obliged to augment representation through these alternative practices. Enhancing representational levels may well have to be deliberately facilitated by such international organizations as the United Nations, agencies like the Commonwealth of Nations, and the governments of major diplomatic powers, including the United States.

Should the Department of State wish to play a leading role in promoting international diplomacy, particularly by helping current and future microstates extend their diplomatic horizons and resolve their representational requirements, it would do well to develop and normalize these augmentative alternatives to traditional bilateral representation. It would need to assist in training the diplomatic personnel of the smaller states (especially new microstates that lack international experience), to establish facilities for consultation, negotiation, and other interchange, and to oversee the creation and operation of communications links between resident missions and their home governments. New forms of credentials could be devised to bridge the gap between the "full power" for ad hoc negotiation and the customary formal "letter of credence," [40] but they would require international recognition. The result, though short of universal interchange of missions among all states, could help to improve diplomatic relations and yet remain within the realm of practicality.

---

[40] For discussion of diplomatic credentials and for copies of appointment and accreditation documents, together with U.S. procedures, see Plischke, *Conduct of American Diplomacy*, pp. 295-297 and Appendices IX-XI, XIII, and XVI-XVII, and Elmer Plischke, *International Relations: Basic Documents*, 2nd ed. (Princeton: Van Nostrand, 1962), Chapter 2. These have also been reproduced in Robert B. Harmon, *The Art and Practice of Diplomacy: A Selected and Annotated Guide* (Metuchen, N.J.: Scarecrow Press, 1971), pp. 229-233, 240.

Potential Diplomatic Community

To appreciate the extent of the diplomatic mission and manpower problem of smaller states, particularly the microstates, and to assess and plan for the future interrelations of all states, it is essential to consider the potential increase in the scope of diplomatic representation. There are at present approximately 6,400 diplomatic missions, or an average of 43 per state. For comparison, if every independent government today commissioned an emissary to every other state, there would be more than 24,000 embassies [41] accredited to 155 governments throughout the world.[42] Should each of these governments also send resident missions to 15 international organizations, the total number of diplomatic establishments would be about 26,000. Supposing all of these missions consisted of an average of 10 officials, each government would function through a corps of some 1,700 diplomats abroad and the participants in the world diplomatic community would exceed a quarter of a million.

Representational missions, naturally, vary considerably in size. For example, in 1975 those accredited to Sierra Leone averaged less than five persons [43] and those to Cyprus about seven,[44] in contrast to

[41]The term *embassy* is used generically to include embassies, legations, and other permanent missions and liaison offices accredited to national governments. Although in earlier times it was not uncommon for states to accredit legations, headed by ministers, to other countries, during and since World War II most of these were elevated to embassy status. In 1975, however, seventeen countries (all European and Latin American except for Indonesia, Saudi Arabia, and Turkey) still maintained seventy legations (1.1 percent of the total number of missions). Two of these were large states (Brazil and Indonesia). On the other hand, only five of the seventeen were smaller states, none of which were microstates, and in only two cases were missions accredited to microstates at the ministerial level (Indonesia to Vatican City, and Yugoslavia to Iceland). It appears, therefore, that historical precedent and national prestige are more influential than population size in determining the level of diplomatic missions and representation. Although the United States maintained all of its missions below the embassy level until the late nineteenth century, currently all of its missions are embassies. For a historical analysis of the level of U.S. missions, see Plischke, *U.S. Diplomats and Their Missions*, pp. 87-97 and Table A-14, pp. 192-197.

[42] By way of comparison, had there been universal bilateral exchange, the number of embassies would have been approximately 1,600 in 1900 and 5,000 in 1940.

[43] Not counting the nine countries that deal with Sierra Leone through multiple appointees who are simultaneously also accredited to, and resident in, neighboring countries. Mission size varied from two persons (for countries like Italy, Spain, and Sweden) to fifteen (the People's Republic of China); Canada had a staff of nine, and France, the Soviet Union, the United Kingdom, and the United States maintained missions of eight members. Information based on Sierra Leone, *Diplomatic and Consular List*.

[44] Embassies varied from two persons to highs of twenty (Turkey) and twenty-three (Soviet Union), and nine other countries, including the United States, main-

fifteen persons per mission in the United States. Nearly thirty governments have mission staffs of twenty-five or more stationed in Washington,[45] but the embassies of twenty other governments consist of only one to three persons.[46] In terms of population categories, the large states (categories G to J) accredit missions to the United States that average some forty-three individuals, while those of small states (categories A to D) average eight persons; the microstates average four. It is only natural that the needs and resources of smaller states dictate smaller missions.

With the increase in functional issues, the intensification of international problems, the bureaucratization of the diplomatic process, the training of requisite personnel, and the improvement of communications facilities abroad, the established trend is for both the quantity of diplomatic missions per country and the size of their staffs to increase. For example, from 1974 to 1975 forty-four states, almost one in three, expanded their diplomatic representation, for a combined increase of some 280 additional missions.[47] In some cases the increase was due to a major change in the government, as in Chile and Spain, or a shift in official policy respecting diplomatic representation, but in most instances it simply reflected accommodation to the enlargement of the family of nations and other natural growth.

Except in the event of war, the severance of diplomatic relations, or the amalgamation of states, it is rare for a country to reduce the quantity of its overseas missions. In the case of the two Chinas, however, as the representational relations of the People's Republic increase, the nationalist government (Taiwan) suffers an offsetting decline, unless Peking and Taipei permit the continuance of relations through liaison or other special types of diplomatic establishments.

Should the international community expand to 300 members, and should each government accredit missions to all others, the diplomatic community could number 90,000, and if each mission averaged 10 members, the population of the diplomatic fraternity would mushroom to 900,000. If each state commissioned resident missions of similar size to a dozen international organizations, supported by foreign offices and servicing agencies that averaged 100 persons, this

tained missions ranging between eleven and sixteen members. Information based on Cyprus, *List of the Diplomatic Corps in Cyprus.*

[45] The most numerous include the Soviet Union (102), the United Kingdom (78), Japan (61), the Federal Republic of Germany (59), the Republic of China (57), Canada (49), Australia (48), France (48), and the Republic of Korea (47).

[46] Such as Botswana, Fiji, Luxembourg, Malta, Upper Volta, and the Yemen.

[47] Figures are based on tabulations provided by *The Statesman's Year Book, 1974-1975* and *1975-1976.*

would increase the international diplomatic community by another 66,000. Each country then would have to maintain a diplomatic corps abroad that numbered more than 3,000, scarcely conceivable for many existing and potential microstates.

Nevertheless, should these averages be achieved, the international diplomatic corps would approach the staggering aggregate of nearly a million diplomats. Although the likelihood of such massive proliferation is not very great at this time, the foreseeable problems are still sufficiently serious to suggest either retarding the growing movement for independence or perfecting and expanding of the use of workable alternatives to traditional bilateral representation, or both. The United States would be well advised to frame its policy on the basis of the changing realities and potential problems in international relations rather than relying upon preexisting custom.

Policy Issues

Because states are naturally selective in their relations, and because they may employ alternatives to traditional bilateral exchange for maintaining direct official contacts with other countries, representational diplomacy, at least superficially, may appear to pose few difficulties for either the global family or its members. However, extensive proliferation of participants, particularly of isolated insular and other microstates, engenders new problems for which policy solutions must be found.

If the smaller states are not able to increase substantially the breadth of their diplomatic effort, they are likely to concentrate their representation upon those larger and nearby powers that are most important to them. As nations proliferate, the degree of nonrepresentation is bound to increase, particularly in the interrelations of the smaller countries. This development would evoke a number of basic questions: Is the community of nations prepared to live with a relative decline in the degree of regularized bilateral diplomatic exchange? Are alternative methods likely to parallel or supplant traditional diplomatic exchanges? Would this undermine the diplomatic process and the interrelations of states? How serious would it be, and how could it be ameliorated?

Aside from commissioning occasional special missions, the problem of the smaller states could be resolved by limiting their direct bilateral representation and resorting to the alternative methods discussed earlier. The larger powers will need to decide the extent to which they are willing to assume the burden of unilateral representation to the proliferating smaller entities. They also will need to consider and respond to such questions as how many small states, like Nauru or Luxembourg, are prepared to commission the governments of other countries to handle their diplomatic representation for them; how far they will go in appointing joint and simultaneous multiple emissaries; and to what extent they can satisfy their representational requirements at major neutral diplomatic centers. These alternative processes can be made to serve useful purposes, but each of them is fraught with difficulties and disadvantages.

The smaller powers are confronted with such fundamental policy issues as whether to live with minimal representation, to expand their diplomatic communities, or to aspire to universality, and which representational processes, and in what combination, they will develop to accommodate their needs. They will then have to determine whether and how to institutionalize their diplomatic effort. Inasmuch as no particular representational alternative or combination is likely to be universally acceptable, the community of nations will be confronted with a pattern of diplomatic interchange that is characterized by diversity, complexity, uncertainty, and fluidity.

This problem of diplomatic representation transcends the interests, requirements, and capacities of the smaller countries. Other states and the aggregate community of nations also need to consider basic policy issues. The United States, other larger powers, and some of the medium-sized countries that now maintain widespread diplomatic representation must decide whether to accept unregulated proliferation and continue their extension of normal diplomatic representation to more and more diminutive entities, perhaps increasingly on a unilateral or simultaneous multiple representation basis, whether to turn to other alternatives, or whether to relinquish the principle of universal diplomatic representation. In short, should the United States be ready to accredit ambassadors to, and, more importantly, establish embassies in Brunei, Dominica, Gibraltar, St. Helena, and the Tokelau Islands?

Continued proliferation will confront the international community with an increasing number of states that have little or no need to deal with each other bilaterally on many matters, or only occasionally on others. This suggests turning more and more to large-scale, multilateral forums for the collective treatment of the universal issues and providing the smaller states with facilities for corridor bipartite discussions and negotiations among themselves. Selected national diplomatic centers may also be induced to furnish such service. In either case, policy decisions will have to be made concerning the nature, extent, and financing of the arrangements. The smaller states, the chief beneficiaries if such facilities are established, may be required to assume the financial costs, but this arrangement may well prove to be less expensive and more rewarding than other representational processes. Many facets of the problem of diplomatic relations may be decided for the United States by other governments, and others may not be regarded as important, but some will need to be faced eventually. The earlier and more definitively they are considered and decided on their merit, the more systematic will be the eventuating policy and practice.

5

TREATY-MAKING AND INTERNATIONAL CONFERENCES

While not necessarily a definitive barometer of its participation in international affairs, a state's engagement in the treaty-making and international conferences of the family of nations serves as a general guideline to its community interest and degree of involvement in world relations. Appendix A specifies the number of bilateral treaties with the United States that each state is a party to and the extent to which each state subscribes to fifty selected basic multilateral treaties and conventions.[1] It also indicates the state's participation in forty-five general international conferences.

Some states tend to be universalistic, engaging generously in both treaty relations and international conferences. Although they determine each involvement individually, they are basically positive and cooperative in their attitude and constructive in their concern for the welfare of the global community. Other states function quite differently, joining minimally except in those treaties and conferences that they regard as being of particular interest and substantial benefit to them. Between these extremes lie the majority of states, which participate in varying ways, so that their selectivity may differ from functional topic to topic, from group to group, and from time to time. Within these general categorizations, states differ considerably in their willingness to reduce relations to formalized commitments and their desire to play an active role, and over the years they may change their attitude concerning the intensity of their involvement.

---

[1] The terms *treaty*, *agreement*, and *convention* are used generically and synonymously in this analysis.

Bilateral Treaties with the United States

The members of the community of nations are party to some 3,300 bilateral treaties and agreements with the United States.[2] It would seem obvious that those states that have the most extensive common interests would also possess the highest treaty relationship. It might also be supposed that the major treaty partners of the United States would be predominantly neighboring countries, world powers, and friendly allies, and that in addition to newness, such factors as smallness, geographic location, and proximity bear a direct relationship to bilateral treaty relations. By and large, these expectations can be validated—subject, however, to significant exceptions.

Table 5 indicates the number and ratio of states with which the United States has bilateral treaties.[3] The United States is party to such treaties with 135 of 154 countries—for an average of approximately 88 percent—and only three population categories (A, B, and J) fall below this ratio, including the microstates.[4] Of the nineteen states that have no bipartite treaties with the United States, eight are of recent origin (emerging in 1974 and 1975) and seven are microstates.[5] As most of these diminutive countries are also recently independent, and a majority of the microstates have some bilateral treaty relations with Washington, it appears that newness is more significant than smallness in explaining the lack of treaty participation.[6] However, in the case of certain older entities—such as Bhutan, Mongolia, the Soviet republics (Byelorussia and the Ukraine), and the People's Republic of China—other reasons pertain.

---

[2] In 1975 there were 3,311.

[3] The concepts of treaty participation and approval are used interchangeably to mean that the states ratified, acceded to, adhered to, or otherwise formally acted to become a party to the treaty or agreement. In some cases a newly emerging state, having previously had a treaty made applicable to it by the metropolitan administering state, becomes bound by the treaty at independence through the deposit of a "notification of succession." Such procedural differences are not material to this study, which is concerned simply with the fact of treaty application.

[4] The participation averages for both the large and medium-sized states (population categories E to J) are 92 percent, the small states (categories C and D) average 90 percent, and the microstates (categories A and B) average 56 percent. Population category J also registers below the overall average because the People's Republic of China (one of three states in this category) has no bilateral treaties with the United States.

[5] The microstates are the Cape Verde Islands, Comoro Islands, Equatorial Guinea, the Maldives, Qatar, São Tomé and Príncipe, and the United Arab Emirates.

[6] This is also verified by experience with larger states, such as newly independent Angola, Mozambique, Papua New Guinea, and Surinam.

62

Table 5
PARTICIPATION IN TREATIES AND INTERNATIONAL CONFERENCES

Popula-tion Category	Number of Nations [a]	Bilateral Treaties with United States			Multilateral Treaties (50 selected)		Multilateral International Conferences (45 selected)		
		Nations with treaties [b]	Number of treaties [b]	Average number of treaties per state	Total participation in treaties [c]	Average per state	Partici-pating nations	Confer-ences attended [d]	Average number of conferences attended
Micro									
A	5	4	21	4.2	66	13.2	4	26	6.5
B	11	5	79	7.2	129	11.7	8	44	5.5
Small									
C	16	14	158	9.9	377	23.6	16	106	6.6
D	47	43	701	14.9	1,179	25.1	46	812	17.7
Medium									
E	50	46	1,217	24.3	1,470	29.4	48	1,204	25.1
F	13	12	538	41.4	424	32.6	13	430	33.1
Large									
G	6	6	332	55.3	208	34.7	6	144	24.0
H	1	1	58	58.0	39	39.0	1	44	44.0
I	2	2	116	58.0	60	30.0	2	59	29.5
J	4	2	91	30.3	128	25.6	4	126	31.5
Total	155	135	3,311	21.5	4,080	26.3	148	2,995	20.2

a From Table 2A.
b Based on Appendix A. No treaties with eight new states (1974-1975); no treaties with eleven other states.
c Based on Appendix A and Table 9.
d Based on Appendix A and Table 10.

More revealing are the quantity and functional subjects of treaties engaged in by individual countries, and by groups of states, according to population size. The average number of treaties per country for the states in bilateral treaty relationship with the United States is about twenty-five. However, as indicated in Table 5, the medium and large population categories approach or exceed the average, but all of the small-state categories (A to D) drop below this level, and the microstates appear at the bottom of the scale.[7]

By and large, the quantity of treaties per country appears to be equatable with population size. That is to say, the larger states generally become involved in more mutual relations with the United States or need to cope with more common problems that require regularization by mutual agreement, as illustrated by Table 6. Only two microstates are parties to more than twenty treaties;[8] a substantial majority have but one or two treaties, or none at all, with the United States.[9] Sixty-four countries (nearly 40 percent of the community of nations) average ten treaties or less, and forty-two, about two-thirds of these low-level participants, are small states. On the other hand, except for Bangladesh, the People's Republic of China, and Nigeria,[10] each of the large states (categories G to J) subscribes to more than thirty treaties, and all of the states that are parties to fifty or more treaties with the United States are medium or large in population size.

Within these broad generalizations considerable variation exists, suggesting that factors other than newness and size also influence treaty participation. It may not be surprising that U.S. bilateral treaty relations are limited with such countries as Albania, Algeria, the

---

[7] The nine microstates having bilateral relations with the United States average about eleven treaties each.

[8] Iceland (thirty-two treaties) and the Bahamas (twenty-five treaties). In addition, Barbados has eighteen and Grenada, independent in 1974, already had twelve by the following year. One reason for the relatively larger number of treaties among former British and certain other Commonwealth colonial territories is that arrangements were made for treaty application in advance of independence. This was the case with the Bahamas, Barbados, Grenada, Guyana, and Nauru. For statements on such treaty succession, see Department of State, *Treaties in Force . . . 1975*, pp. 14, 17, 109, 115, and 186-187. When certain other British territories gained independence, stipulations were agreed to that the new state assumed all international obligations and responsibilities of the United Kingdom insofar as they applied to the new country. For examples pertaining to Cyprus and Malta, see *Treaties in Force . . . 1975*, pp. 64 and 176-177.

[9] These include Bahrain, Nauru, and Western Samoa—two each, Vatican City—one, and seven states with no treaties (see note 5).

[10] Nigeria has eleven treaties, Bangladesh has six, and Communist China has none.

Table 6

U.S. BILATERAL TREATY RELATIONS, SUMMARY BY POPULATION CATEGORY

Number of Treaties	Population Category										Total Countries
	A	B	C	D	E	F	G	H	I	J	
None	1	6	2	4	4	1	0	0	0	1	19
1–10	3	2	6	18	15	0	1	0	0	0	45
11–20	1	1	6	11	9	1	1	0	0	0	30
21–30	0	1	2	7	8	3	0	0	0	0	21
31–40	0	1	0	4	5	1	1	0	1	0	13
41–50	0	0	0	3	4	2	0	0	0	2	11
More than 50	0	0	0	0	5	5	3	1	1	0	15
Total countries	5	11	16	47	50	13	6	1	2	3	154

Source: Compiled from Appendix A.

Democratic Republic of Germany, Libya and Oman,[11] or that, despite the fact that three of the older African powers have active treaty relations with the United States,[12] half of the sub-Saharan African countries, in part because of their newness, are party to an average of less than three treaties.

Such factors as immediate and regional proximity and collective defense partnership as well as other special forms of association are understandably reflected in bilateral treaty relations. In the Western Hemisphere, Canada has the record number of treaties and agreements with the United States—186. Mexico has 64, and Panama has 45. Some of the older European powers, with which the United States has dealt diplomatically for many years, also have a high ratio—led by the United Kingdom (128), West Germany (79), France (69), Italy (68), Greece (64), and the Netherlands (57). The overall European average is 35, but the quota for the East European states is only 25. The fourteen North Atlantic Alliance powers have more than 900 bipartite treaties with the United States, an average of 65 per

---

[11] The figures are: Albania (six treaties), Libya (three), Oman (two), and Algeria and the Democratic Republic of Germany (one each).

[12] Liberia (thirty treaties), Ethiopia (twenty-seven), and South Africa (twenty). A few of the newer African countries also have active treaty records, including Zaire (nineteen), Ghana (eighteen), and Sierra Leone (sixteen).

country,[13] although this includes four smaller states.[14] American bilateral allies in Asia and the Western Pacific—Australia, the Republic of China, South Korea, Japan, New Zealand, and the Philippines—have approximately 360 treaties, for an average of 60.[15] On the other hand, the average for the twenty traditional Latin American countries is 33 treaties, and for the seven recent Caribbean states, 17. A comparison of the records of these geographic groupings with overall global tendencies makes it clear that historical association, alliance partnership, and ideological identity—or differences—significantly influence bilateral treaty affairs.

It also is interesting to note that treaty relationship with the United States tends to be higher for island and coastal states than for those that are landlocked. This does not apply to some of the older, established European powers—such as Austria, Czechoslovakia, Hungary, Luxembourg, and Switzerland—or to Paraguay, all of which except Czechoslovakia are party to more than twenty treaties.[16] Some nineteen other landlocked states average only 4.5 treaties, however. Twelve of these are post-World War II sub-Saharan African countries,[17] but the group also includes Afghanistan, Jordan, and Nepal, as well as several countries that have no bilateral treaties with the United States, including Mongolia and the two Soviet republics. The seacoast factor is illustrated by the treaty relations of the United States with European powers, for which the average is forty treaties for the littoral and only twenty-five for the landlocked states.[18] Nevertheless, the record suggests that newness, the general intensity of international relations, and occasionally ideological differences are primarily responsible for disparities in the quantity of U.S. bipartite

---

[13] This includes Canada, and if it is excluded from the computation, the European North Atlantic powers still average fifty-six treaties.

[14] Denmark, Iceland, Luxembourg, and Norway.

[15] The Philippine Republic accounts for the largest number (eighty-nine).

[16] Austria (thirty-seven treaties), Paraguay (thirty-six), Hungary (twenty-seven), Luxembourg (twenty-two), Switzerland (twenty-one), and Czechoslovakia (seventeen).

[17] However, since the overall average for twenty-seven coastal post-World War II sub-Saharan African states is only 6.3, it may be that, in this instance, newness and other factors are equally contributory.

[18] This may also be explained, in part, by the extended U.S. treaty record with a substantial number of friendly European states and close interrelations with them since World War II, and by the comparative smallness of Luxembourg and postwar difficulties with the East European Communist countries. Coastal location does not appear to be a factor for U.S. relations with the countries of the Western Hemisphere, where the general average (exclusive of Canada) is twenty-nine, and the two landlocked South American states (Bolivia and Paraguay) exceed this ratio.

agreements as between coastal and landlocked countries. So far as specific treaty subjects are concerned, the most significant distinction reflects the absence of commitments with landlocked states concerning fishery, navigation, and other maritime affairs.

Table 7 specifies thirty-eight functional subject categories of U.S. bilateral treaties[19] and indicates their applicability to all of the small states (categories A to D) and, for comparative purposes, to twenty-five other selected countries—generally larger, older, more active, or neighboring states.[20] From the totals shown in Table 7, it may be seen that approximately three-fourths of the treaties participated in by the seventy-nine small states fall into twelve categories (given in descending numerical sequence): defense and mutual security (125 treaties), agriculture and commodities (91), economic and technical assistance (67), finance and investment guarantees (59), transport and communications (59), aviation and outer space (56), extradition (44), trade and commerce (43), visas (42), postal affairs (41), the Peace Corps (40), and taxation (38). These categories are also the source of numerous treaties with the larger states (see totals, Table 6), although the sequence differs somewhat in that treaties dealing with aviation and space, extradition, trade and commerce, visas, and especially the Peace Corps register lower in their frequency scale. The larger powers also participate in a much higher ratio of treaties dealing not only with maritime and navigation, atomic and nuclear energy, and claims matters, but also, strangely, with aid and assistance.

Noteworthy is the fact that, while the microstates' bilateral treaty relations with the United States generally comport with the record of other small states (categories C and D), half of their treaties fall into only five subject categories—defense and mutual security, agriculture and commodities, postal affairs, aviation and outer space, and

---

[19] This grouping is based largely on functional category designations used in Department of State, *Treaties in Force*. The treaties listed in the last category, designated "others," include occasional agreements dealing with embassy sites (U.S.S.R.), energy (U.S.S.R.), exterritoriality (Republic of China), insular possessions (United Kingdom), judicial procedure (West Germany, Panama, Sierra Leone, and Spain), marriage (Italy), migratory birds (Canada, Japan, and Mexico), nuclear war (U.S.S.R.), pollution (Canada), rules of warfare (Nicaragua and Panama), stolen property (Mexico), whaling (Japan), and other miscellaneous matters.

[20] Argentina, Austria, Belgium, Brazil, Canada, the People's Republic of China, the Republic of China, France, the Federal Republic of Germany, Greece, India, Indonesia, Iran, Italy, Japan, Mexico, the Netherlands, Pakistan, Poland, Portugal, Spain, Sweden, Turkey, the U.S.S.R., and the United Kingdom. Ten of these are large, and fifteen are medium-sized states. Because of their low number of bilateral treaties with the United States, two large states (Bangladesh and Nigeria) are not included.

Table 7

U.S. BILATERAL TREATY PARTICIPATION, BY SUBJECT AND POPULATION CATEGORY

Treaty Subjects	Small states					Twenty-five selected larger states [a]						
Population Category	A	B	C	D	Total	E	F	G	H	I	J	Total
Agriculture and Commodities [b]	0	10	3	78	91	24	40	11	7	13	10	105
Aid and Assistance	0	1	2	12	15	15	15	10	1	0	4	45
Atomic and Nuclear Energy [b]	0	0	0	8	8	16	6	7	4	1	4	38
Aviation, Outer Space, and Satellites [b][c]	1	5	11	39	56	29	22	30	4	6	5	96
Boundaries	0	0	0	3	3	32	13	12	0	0	0	57
Canal Rights	0	0	0	4	4	0	0	1	0	0	0	1
Claims	0	0	2	0	2	10	3	13	1	4	2	33
Consular Affairs [b]	2	3	11	8	24	6	3	3	0	2	2	16
Copyright [b]	0	0	0	1	1	1	2	4	1	0	1	9
Customs and Smuggling [b]	0	1	0	14	15	12	6	4	1	2	0	25
Defense and Mutual Security	0	19	12	94	125	93	35	70	6	26	3	233
Drugs and Narcotic Drugs [b]	0	0	0	4	4	6	11	3	0	2	0	22
Economic and Technical Cooperation [d]	0	5	12	50	67	16	12	10	4	5	4	51
Education and Cultural Affairs [b]	0	1	2	11	14	9	6	6	1	2	2	26
Extradition	3	3	12	26	44	11	5	5	1	3	2	26
Finance and Investment Guarantees [b]	1	2	13	43	59	18	11	15	1	8	5	58
Fisheries	0	0	0	1	1	8	1	1	1	4	6	21
General and Amity	0	0	0	10	10	4	5	3	7	0	6	13
Maritime and Navigation [b][e]	1	0	0	7	7	43	12	15	7	4	3	84
Meteorology and Weather Stations	0	2	1	5	9	4	1	2	0	0	3	7
Military Affairs [b]	0	0	2	0	2	3	3	2	0	0	0	8
Military Missions (Army, Navy, Air)	0	0	0	14	14	3	3	0	1	0	0	7

											Total
Nationality	0	0	0	12	12	4	1	0	0	0	0	5
Occupied Territories	0	0	0	3	3	2	2	1	0	0	1	6
Pacific Settlement of Disputes [b]	0	2	11	16	20	16	5	6	2	0	1	30
Patents and Trademarks	2	2	0	9	24	10	5	9	1	1	1	27
Peace	0	2	0	0	0	0	2	4	0	0	0	6
Peace Corps	2	3	13	22	40	0	2	1	1	1	1	6
Postal Affairs [b]	3	6	9	23	41	19	7	6	1	3	2	38
Property (including Surplus Property) [b]	1	2	10	9	22	9	5	7	0	3	1	25
Publications and Information Media [b]	0	1	0	18	19	4	7	4	1	3	1	20
Scientific Cooperation [f]	0	0	0	13	13	5	6	2	2	1	6	22
Social Security	0	0	1	2	3	2	3	2	0	0	0	7
Taxation	1	4	5	28	38	28	7	11	1	3	0	50
Trade and Commerce	1	0	6	36	43	28	11	17	2	6	4	68
Transport and Communications [b g]	1	4	6	48	59	26	7	6	2	1	5	47
Visas	2	3	12	25	42	10	7	6	2	3	2	30
Others	0	0	0	5	5	16	9	4	2	8	16	55
Total	21	79	158	701	959	542	301	315	58	116	91	1,423

[a] Includes larger, older, and neighboring states from population categories E-J: Argentina, Austria, Belgium, Brazil, Canada, People's Republic of China, Republic of China, France, Federal Republic of Germany, Greece, India, Indonesia, Iran, Italy, Japan, Mexico, Netherlands, Pakistan, Poland, Portugal, Spain, Sweden, Turkey, U.S.S.R., and the United Kingdom.

[b] Also see multilateral treaties, Table 9.

[c] Includes atmospheric sampling, remote sensing, space research, and tracking stations.

[d] Includes Lend-Lease and mutual assistance.

[e] Includes inland navigation.

[f] Includes geodetic surveying, mapping, and oceanographic and seismological research.

[g] Includes automotive traffic, highways, and telecommunications.

Source: U.S. Department of State, *Treaties in Force . . . January 1, 1975* (Washington, D.C.: Government Printing Office, Department of State Publication 8798, 1975), pp. 3-301.

extradition; those concerned with financial and trade matters are less numerous. Moreover, the microstates have no treaties with the United States in nearly half of the functional categories, including such matters as atomic and nuclear energy, drugs, fishery, military, and maritime affairs.

In general, it may be concluded that the microstates fall well below the overall standard of bipartite treaty participation with the United States. Size, therefore, appears to be a critical factor in such treaty involvement. However, in some cases newness, historical association, and geographic location may be even more important. In view of their limited population size, and their national interests and needs, it is reasonable to assume that the microstates are not apt to become as active in treaty participation as the larger states. Nevertheless, size may be less of a factor than their attitude respecting their status as independent states and their sense of obligation in fulfilling national responsibilities as members of the community of nations.[21]

Selected Multilateral Treaties

To complement analysis of bipartite agreements, it is equally important to examine the extent of participation in multilateral treaties. For this purpose, fifty treaties have been selected that are unrestricted geographically, are intended to be continuing if not permanent, and would be expected, because they are law-creating, rule-making, service-arranging, and rights-protecting, to possess widespread appeal and significance. Several of these antedate World War II and remain in effect, some have grown out of U.N. action, and all are intended to gain universal endorsement. Collectively, they constitute a substantial and representative core of existing multipartite treaties and conventions that should be of considerable interest and value to a broad spectrum of states—old or new, large or small, industrialized or developing.[22]

---

[21] It is not feasible in this review to assess the degree to which U.S. initiative, as compared with that of individual microstates, influences their bilateral treaty participation. For example, it is conceivable that agreements on such matters as defense and mutual security, outer space, patents and trademarks, and extradition were prompted by Washington, while agreements on agriculture and commodities, postal and communications affairs, and the granting of visas are of equal concern to the microstate, and may initiate with it.

[22] It should be noted that basic treaties serving as the constitutive acts of the United Nations and other international organizations are not included in this list; they are dealt with separately in the following chapter.

Participation in multilateral treaty relations is indicated for each member of the community of nations in Appendix A, is summarized by population category in Table 5, and is itemized by treaty and population category in Table 9. The total possible participation of 155 states in the fifty multipartite treaties would be 7,750; the actual level of ratification is 4,080 (53 percent).[23] The average number of treaties participated in tends to increase according to population size.[24] The overall average is 26.5 treaties per country. All of the medium and large population categories exceed this level, and the four groups of small states all fall below it. The fact that the microstates average only 12.2 treaties, or less than half of the overall ratio,[25] generally confirms the nonparticipation revealed in their low level of engagement in bipartite treaties with the United States. Smallness, therefore, is clearly a factor in a state's participation in the affairs of the world community.

As with bilateral treaties, the precise degree of treaty involvement by individual states and other factors may be more important than any simple aggregate survey. For example, six states are not party to any of these fifty treaties and another seven subscribe to only five or less; but of these thirteen states, nine became independent in 1974 and 1975 and therefore had little opportunity to ratify them. On the other hand, only three of these minimal participants are microstates,[26] whereas four microstates are party to twenty treaties or more.[27] Not counting the three new ones, microstates ratified on the average of fifteen of the multilateral treaties, as compared with the overall ratio of 26.5.

No state has ratified all of the fifty multipartite treaties. Forty-one states (26 percent) are party to twenty or less, ninety-one (59

---

[23] As of January 1, 1975. This computation does not include the seventy-nine ratifications of these fifty treaties by other entities, including the European principalities (Liechtenstein, Monaco, and San Marino—forty-eight), the former Baltic states (Estonia, Latvia, and Lithuania—twenty-five), and Danzig (four), Brunei (one), and Southern Rhodesia (one).

[24] Category A—13.2 treaties; B—11.7; C—23.6; D—25.1; E—29.4; F—32.6; G—34.7; H—39.0; I—30.0; J—32.0.

[25] This amounts to only 24 percent of their potential—that is, the maximum quantity of participation possible by the microstates.

[26] The Cape Verde Islands, Comoro Islands, and São Tomé and Príncipe—all independent in 1975.

[27] The Bahamas (twenty), Tonga (twenty-three), Barbados (twenty-eight), and Iceland (thirty-four). Six other microstates are party to seven to nine of these treaties (Bahrain, Equatorial Guinea, the Maldives, Qatar, the United Arab Emirates, and Western Samoa), and three have subscribed to twelve to eighteen (Nauru—twelve, Grenada—thirteen, and Vatican City—eighteen).

Table 8

MULTILATERAL TREATY PARTICIPATION, SUMMARY BY POPULATION CATEGORY

Number of Treaties	Population Category										Total Countries
	A	B	C	D	E	F	G	H	I	J	
None	1	2	1	0	2	0	0	0	0	0	6
1–10	0	6	2	2	2	0	1	0	0	1	14
11–20	3	1	0	12	4	1	0	0	0	0	21
21–30	1	1	8	24	19	4	0	0	1	0	58
31–40	0	1	5	5	12	5	2	1	1	1	33
41–50	0	0	0	4	11	3	3	0	0	2	23
Total countries	5	11	16	47	50	13	6	1	2	4	155

Source: Compiled from Appendix A.

percent) subscribe to twenty-one to forty, and twenty-three[28] (15 percent) have ratified more than forty, as indicated in Table 8. All but five of the highest-level participants are European powers, with Denmark, Norway, the United Kingdom, and Finland heading the list.[29] The United States is party to forty-five,[30] and the other non-European powers that have ratified forty or more are Australia, Canada, Mexico, and New Zealand.[31]

Naturally, states differ in their concern with the various functional subjects covered by multipartite treaties. Examination of treaty application reveals not only key world issues and the general appeal of their resolution by international accord but also the degree of support a given agreement receives from various types of countries, including microstates. Table 9, which lists the fifty selected multi-

[28] These twenty-three include not only the major Western and industrialized powers but also several East European Communist states—Hungary (forty), Romania (forty), the Soviet Union (forty-four), and Yugoslavia (forty-five).

[29] The figures are: Denmark (forty-eight), Norway and the United Kingdom (forty-seven each), and Finland (forty-six).

[30] The United States has not ratified or acceded to conventions on gas and bacteriological warfare (1925), genocide (1948), elimination of racial discrimination (1965), and human rights—civil and political (1966), and economic, social, and cultural (1966).

[31] In addition to Bangladesh (five treaties) and the People's Republic of China (five), the populous states that fall below this level of participation are Brazil (thirty-nine), Nigeria (thirty-eight), India (thirty-six), Pakistan (thirty-four), and Indonesia (twenty-two).

Table 9

PARTICIPATION IN INDIVIDUAL MULTILATERAL TREATIES, BY POPULATION CATEGORY, 1975[a]

Treaty Subject	A (5)	B (11)	C (16)	D (47)	E (50)	F (13)	G (6)	H (1)	I (2)	J (4)	Total (155)
War and Arms Control Treaties[c]											
Biological and Toxin Weapons, 1972	0	4	11	33	40	12	5	1	2	3	111
Civilians in Time of War—Protection of, 1949	2	6	15	43	47	12	6	1	2	4	138
Gas and Bacteriological Warfare,[d] 1925	2	4	12	25	35	11	5	1	2	3	100
Nuclear Nonproliferation, 1968	2	3	12	35	36	9	4	0	2	2	105
Nuclear Test Ban, 1963	2	2	11	40	43	12	5	1	2	3	121
Opening of Hostilities, 1907	0	0	1	12	14	7	3	1	1	3	42
Prisoners of War, 1949	2	6	15	44	48	13	6	1	2	4	141
Renunciation of War (Pact of Paris), 1928	0	2	2	14	26	9	3	1	1	3	61
Seabed Arms Control, 1971	0	2	8	34	34	7	3	1	1	3	93
War—Rules of (Hague Conventions), 1899/1907	0	0	1	14	24	8	4	1	1	3	56
Other Treaties[c]											
Air—International Transportation, 1929	3	4	12	30	39	8	5	1	3	3	108
Air Services—Transit, 1944	0	4	10	28	27	11	4	0	1	2	87
Arbitration—Enforcement of Awards, 1958	0	0	2	8	18	8	3	0	1	3	43
Astronauts—Rescue of, 1968	1	3	9	14	21	7	4	1	0	2	62
Atlantic Charter, 1941	0	0	1	14	19	8	1	1	0	3	47
Collision at Sea—Prevention of, 1960	0	2	5	13	23	8	5	1	2	3	62

Nations Committed[b] (number of states)

Table 9 (continued)

Treaty Subject	Nations Committed[b] (number of states)										
	A (5)	B (11)	C (16)	D (47)	E (50)	F (13)	G (6)	H (1)	I (2)	J (4)	Total (155)
Consular Relations, 1963	2	0	8	20	25	5	5	1	0	1	67
Continental Shelf, 1958	1	0	7	13	23	6	2	0	0	2	54
Copyright—Universal Convention, 1952	2	2	6	22	26	4	5	1	1	3	72
Customs—Automotive—for Touring, 1954	2	1	8	22	30	7	4	0	1	3	78
Diplomatic Relations, 1961	2	4	13	36	38	9	5	1	2	2	112
Genocide,[d] 1948	1	2	2	22	35	12	4	1	0	2	81
Hijacking of Aircraft, 1970	0	2	5	19	27	9	5	1	1	2	71
Human Rights—Civil and Political,[d] 1966	0	1	2	13	14	2	1	0	0	1	34
Human Rights—Economic, Social, and Cultural,[d] 1966	0	1	2	13	14	3	1	0	0	1	35
Industrial Property, 1911–1967	2	3	5	24	29	8	4	1	2	2	80
Intelstat, 1971	1	2	6	21	37	10	5	1	2	2	87
Life at Sea—Safety of, 1960	1	3	6	25	32	10	5	1	2	3	88
Load Lines, 1966	0	2	5	18	27	9	5	1	1	3	71
Narcotic Drugs, 1912–1961	4	5	13	41	45	13	5	1	2	3	132
Outer Space—Exploration and Use of, 1967	1	2	4	19	25	10	5	1	1	2	70
Pacific Settlement (Hague Conventions), 1899/1907	0	1	4	17	31	9	4	1	1	3	71
Pacific Settlement of Investment Disputes, 1965	0	1	10	24	20	3	5	0	2	1	66
Plant Protection (Agricultural), 1951	1	2	4	23	23	6	4	1	1	3	68
Postal—Universal Convention, 1969	3	8	14	44	45	13	6	1	2	3	139
Publications—International Exchange of, 1958	1	2	4	12	11	5	4	1	1	2	43
Publications—Obscene, 1910	2	4	11	17	30	9	5	1	2	3	84

Treaty											Total
Racial Discrimination—Elimination of,[d] 1965	2	4	9	28	30	8	4	1	0	2	88
Radio Regulations, 1963	2	1	6	24	27	8	5	0	1	3	77
Red Cross, 1929/1949	3	6	15	44	48	13	6	1	2	4	142
Refugees—Status of, 1967	1	1	8	20	18	3	4	1	0	1	57
Road Traffic, 1949	2	4	11	30	35	8	2	0	1	3	96
Slave Trade, 1926	3	4	11	32	37	10	5	1	1	3	107
Slave Traffic—White, 1904	2	3	8	20	29	9	5	1	2	3	82
Slavery and Slave Trade, 1956	3	6	12	24	36	10	5	1	0	3	100
Telecommunication—International Convention, 1965	3	7	14	45	46	13	6	1	2	3	140
Telegraph Regulations, 1958	2	1	3	17	30	12	4	1	2	3	75
Territorial Sea and Contiguous Zone, 1958	1	0	6	8	19	4	3	0	1	2	44
United Nations Declaration, 1942	0	0	1	13	20	8	1	1	0	3	47
Whaling—Regulation of, 1935	2	2	7	8	14	6	3	1	1	1	45
Total	66	129	377	1,179	1,470	424	208	39	60	128	4,080
Percent of participation by population category	1.6	3.2	9.2	28.9	36.0	10.4	5.1	1.0	1.5	3.1	100.0
Average for states per population category	13.2	11.7	23.6	25.1	29.4	32.6	34.7	39.0	30.0	32.0	

a Does not include constitutive acts of international organizations (for United Nations and related agencies, see Appendix A) or commodity agreements.

b Figures denote states that have ratified, acceded, or had treaty applied by succession on becoming independent.

c General title of treaty, with date of signature.

d United States has not ratified.

Source: U.S. Department of State, *Treaties in Force . . . January 1, 1975* (Washington, D.C.: Government Printing Office, Department of State Publication 8798, 1975), pp. 305-446; U.S. Arms Control and Disarmament Agency, *Arms Control and Disarmament Agreements: Texts and History of Negotiations* (Washington, D.C.: Government Printing Office, Arms Control and Disarmament Agency Publication 77, 1975); for treaties not ratified by the United States, information was obtained from the Treaty Affairs Office of the Department of State.

lateral treaties with their dates of signature, provides aggregate participation statistics by population categories. Ten treaties dealing with the laws of war and arms control are grouped separately. Overall, these enjoy 62 percent ratification. For the microstates, however, the approval ratio is only 24 percent, whereas the states in the medium and large population categories are party to 72 percent. Pre-World War II agreements concerned with the commencement of hostilities, the general rules of war (Hague Conventions), and the renunciation of war (Paris Peace Pact) rate relatively low endorsement, while those concerned with arms control possess widespread support, and those dealing with the treatment of prisoners of war and of civilians in times of hostilities achieve the highest degree of ratification. Participation of the microstates, aside from their lower level of ratification, conforms with this general pattern.

The forty remaining treaties, which deal with diverse issues, have been approved by an average of seventy-eight states, about one-half of the community of nations. Approval ratios bear a direct relationship to population size, with the microstates lowest, and the large powers achieving the highest ratios. Again the microstates are parties to an average of somewhat less than one treaty in four on the list; large states on the average ratify nearly two of three.[32]

The International Telecommunication (140 states), Postal (139), and Red Cross (142) conventions enjoy virtual universal approval—91 percent overall. Other treaties achieving a high degree of endorsement include those concerned with air transport (108), diplomatic relations (112), narcotic drugs (132), slavery and the slave trade (100 and 107), and road traffic (96); this group averages 70 percent approval.[33] Treaties dealing with transportation and communications (including safety of life at sea, and radio and telegraph regulations), the exploration and use of outer space, the protection of copyright and trademarks, the pacific settlement of disputes (Hague Conventions), and the outlawry or control of aerial hijacking, genocide, obscene publications, and racial discrimination also have received substantial concurrence, ranging from 45 percent to 57 percent. Low ratification rates apply to several treaties which, though still in force, are historically oriented, such as the Atlantic Charter (1941) and the United Nations Declaration (1942), to some concerned with specialized subjects such as whaling, and, surprisingly, to those dealing with the

[32] Approval averages are: microstates—24.4 percent, other small states (categories C and D)—46.6 percent, medium states—57.4 percent, and large states—64.4 percent.

[33] Their individual approval ratios range from 62 to 85 percent.

territorial sea and its contiguous zone, with the enforcement of arbitration awards, and with human rights.[34] Acquiescence ratios for these range from 30 percent down to only 22 percent.

Microstate treaty participation conforms generally with this configuration of high and low approval rates, except that, as a group, the microstates are less supportive of treaties dealing with air transport, copyright, and genocide. One may wonder, however, why they give so little approval to certain treaties that might be regarded as important to diminutive states, such as the Vienna Convention on Diplomatic Relations of 1961 (ratified only by Bahrain, the Bahamas, Barbados, Iceland, Tonga, and Vatican City), the treaty of 1963 on consular relations (only by Tonga and Vatican City), the Hague Conventions of 1899 and 1907 on the pacific settlement of disputes (only by Iceland), and the treaty of 1958 on the continental shelf (only by Tonga).

A number of factors influence the multilateral treaty participation of the microstates. When their ratification record is compared with larger states, as noted, smallness appears to be significant. Because three new microstates (1975) are not party to any of the fifty treaties, newness also may be said to account for lack of participation; but if they are exempted, the microstates that came into being in the 1970s—having an average of 13.3 treaties—are not much less active participants than those that antedate 1970—for which the average is 16.4 treaties. The recency of the treaty may also bear on the degree of acceptance, but this does not appear to be a critical criterion in the list of treaties under consideration. Moreover, factors such as geographic location and proximity to a particular country are less pertinent than they are when dealing with bipartite treaties.

For the global community overall, it seems that fundamental attitude toward the nature and degree of involvement in world affairs and treaty commitment together with the perceived relevancy of the specific subjects and obligations embodied in the treaties are the most significant determinants of participation. This would help explain the high ratification rate of many of the older Western industrialized states, as well, perhaps, as that of such smaller states as Iceland, Jamaica, Luxembourg, Malta, Mauritius, and Trinidad and Tobago—all of which are parties to thirty or more and exceed the degree of involvement of such larger countries as Ethiopia, Nepal, Saudi Arabia,

---

[34] The Human Rights covenants, dealing respectively with civil and political rights, and with economic, social and cultural rights, were opened for signature in 1966, but did not enter into effect until early 1976, when they achieved the required minimum of thirty-five ratifications.

Sudan, and Uganda, which have ratified less than twenty-five, to say nothing of such notoriously reluctant participants as the People's Republic of China (five treaties), North Korea (five), and North Vietnam (three).[35]

Selected Multipartite International Conferences

The extent of a state's participation in international conferences constitutes another basic indicator of its involvement in the affairs of the international community. Governments, perhaps especially those of smaller countries, are attracted by global or other conclaves, finding in them an opportunity to espouse their policy interests and enhance their national image in the international arena. Because attendance also may afford considerable external influence, without exacting prior obligations and at minimum financial cost, normally a high degree of enthusiasm for conferences may be expected, regardless of the size of states.

International conferences are distinguishable on the basis of such criteria as sponsorship, objectives, generality or specificity of agenda, universality of participation, and intended end-products. They may also be differentiated as global or regional, as inclusive or restricted, as regularized or ad hoc, as diplomatic or technical, and as problem-solving, policy-formulating, program-launching, agency-establishing, rule-making, or law-creating. For purposes of analyzing microstate participation, forty-five general multipartite conferences were selected, covering the period from 1943 to 1975. Most of these were presumably intended by their initiators to be universal in membership, and were designed to serve important constitutive purposes (to create global international organizations), as forums for negotiation on broad matters of mutual policy, or to refine elements of international law and practice. They also were expected to evoke widespread interest among independent members of the global community, including the smaller states.

In some respects the conference participation pattern of states resembles that of their engagement in traditional diplomatic representation, in others it parallels their joining with other governments

[35] It should be noted that Byelorussia (twenty-six treaties), the Ukraine (twenty-six), and Mongolia (twenty-one), which have no bilateral treaties with the United States, nevertheless are average participants in the fifty multilateral treaties. The considerable disparity between the ratification level of the Soviet Union (forty-four) and its two republics (twenty-six for Byelorussia and the Ukraine) raises interesting questions.

in treaty relations, and in still others it reflects their affiliation with international organizations. As a barometer of involvement, however, conference attendance differs from the ratification of treaties in that it may depend on being invited by conference sponsors. Moreover, because of the costs of the intensive participation in conferences that has become common contemporary practice, some of the smaller and less endowed countries may be constrained to exercise considerable selectivity, as they do in accrediting diplomatic envoys to foreign capitals and in joining international organizations.

Conference attendance records of individual states are presented in Appendix A, and summary computations by population categories are given in Table 5. The latter indicates that, overall, 148 governments sent 2,995 delegations to the forty-five conferences,[36] averaging an attendance record of approximately twenty conferences per state, and that the participation ratio generally increases in relation to population size. Microstates on average were represented at only six of the forty-five conferences. The ratio for other small countries is fifteen, for medium-sized states is twenty-seven, and for large states approximates twenty-nine.[37] This alignment by population categories is generally confirmed by relating actual to possible conference attendance. The ratio of conferences attended to overall possible participation (if all states had attended the forty-five conferences) amounts to 42.9 percent, and individual population categories range from 08.9 percent (category B) to 97.8 percent (category H). All of the smaller population categories (A to D) fall below the general possibility average, and all of the medium-sized and large population categories (E to J) exceed it. To summarize, the levels of actual to overall possible conference attendance computes to the following:

	Population Categories	Percent of Participation	
Microstates	A and B	09.7	27.8
Other Small States	C and D	32.4	
Medium-sized States	E and F	57.6	58.7
Large States	G to J	63.8	

[36] The statistics in this analysis do not count the international conference attendance of quasi states or national and other observership missions, including: Andorra (two), Bermuda (one), Hong Kong (one), Liechtenstein (eight), Monaco (seventeen), San Marino (twelve), and Southern Rhodesia (six), for a total of forty-seven delegations. The European principalities accounted for 83 percent.
[37] These computations exclude the newer states that attended none of the conferences.

This indicates a direct and significant relationship between population size and conference attendance. However, newness, status during World War II, national attitude toward participation, and other factors are also important and are reflected in the records of individual countries. The older and traditionally active powers have the highest attendance records. Four countries sent missions to all forty-five conferences—Belgium, France, the United Kingdom, and the United States—and seventeen others attended thirty-nine or more. Of these twenty-one countries, all but four are European and Western Hemisphere powers.[38] The relatively low rates of involvement for states like Austria, Germany, Japan, and Spain—none of which exceeds thirty—is due, to some extent, to their lack of participation in the World War II conferences to negotiate the United Nations Charter and the constitutions of other major international organizations.[39]

Of the countries that became independent since World War II, only sixteen attended fifteen or more of these forty-five conferences, and all of these, except Morocco and Tunisia, were created in the 1940s.[40] Among the postwar states, India, Lebanon, Pakistan, and the Philippines attended the largest number (from thirty to forty-two). Other post-World War II states fall below the modest level of fifteen conferences, with such larger countries as the People's Republic of China, the Democratic Republic of Germany, the Democratic People's Republic of Korea, and the Democratic Republic of Vietnam evidencing minimal participation.[41]

---

[38] Ten are European countries (Belgium, Czechoslovakia, Denmark, France, Greece, the Netherlands, Norway, Poland, the United Kingdom, and Yugoslavia), seven are Western Hemisphere powers (Argentina, Brazil, Canada, Chile, Mexico, the United States, and Venezuela), and the remaining four are Australia, Egypt, India, and Turkey. Other states with high levels of participation (thirty-five to thirty-eight conferences) include the Republic of China, Iran, Italy, New Zealand, the Philippines, Sweden, the Soviet Union, and seven Latin American republics. Twenty-seven of these thirty-five most active participants, more than three-fourths, are Western Hemisphere and European powers.

[39] Among the others attending few of the wartime conferences because of their World War II roles were Albania, Bulgaria, Finland, Italy, and Romania. In addition, of the older states, Mongolia was represented at only one conference before 1963.

[40] Burma (nineteen conferences), Iceland (twenty-two), India (forty-two), Indonesia (twenty-nine), Israel (twenty-six), Jordan (fifteen), Khmer Republic (fifteen), the Republic of Korea (nineteen), Lebanon (thirty-two), Morocco (nineteen), Pakistan (thirty), the Philippines (thirty-five), Sri Lanka (twenty-four), Syria (twenty-four), Tunisia (nineteen), and the Republic of Vietnam (nineteen). Though not independent until after World War II, India and the Philippines sent missions regularly to the conferences during the war years.

[41] Their records to 1975 are as follows: Communist China—three conferences, Germany—four, Korea—two, and Vietnam—one, all since 1973.

Low international conference participation is incontestably related to newness as well as to size. Of the seven states that failed to be present at any of these forty-five conferences, six were established in 1975 and had little or no opportunity to become involved.[42] Thirty other countries, the preponderant majority of which came into being since 1965,[43] attended five or less. Of these thirty-seven post-World War II low-level participants, thirty (81 percent) are small in population (categories A to D), of which fourteen (38 percent) are microstates.[44]

Except for Iceland and Vatican City, all of the microstates are minimal conference participants. Despite its small size, Iceland sent delegations to half of the conferences since 1945, and Vatican City, although rarely engaging in international constitutive conclaves (15), accredited delegations to three-fourths of the other conferences (30), attending almost all that were not concerned with the Axis peace treaties, the seas, and commercial aviation. However, in terms of conference potentialities—that is, the ratio between actual and possible attendance—both Iceland and the Vatican are modest participants,[45] whereas a number of other microstates have been more active.[46]

In relation to potential attendance, of the pre-World War II countries other than microstates, as suggested by Appendix A, approximately two-thirds (forty-one states) exceed a 70 percent participation record.[47] Thirty-four post-World War II states have 70 percent or

[42] Angola, Cape Verde Islands, Comoro Islands, Mozambique, Papua New Guinea, and São Tomé and Príncipe. The seventh is the Maldives, in existence since 1965.

[43] Nine antedate 1965: the People's Republic of China, East Germany, North Korea, Malawi, Malta, Somalia, North Vietnam, Western Samoa, and Zambia.

[44] Only seven belong to the larger population categories, including such new countries as Angola, Mozambique, and Bangladesh, and four Communist countries already mentioned—the People's Republic of China, East Germany, North Korea, and North Vietnam. The breakdown of the thirty-seven low participation states is as follows: Category A—four states, B—ten, C and D—sixteen, E and F—five, and G to J—two.

[45] Iceland participated in twenty-one of forty-four (48 percent) conferences since it became independent and Vatican City in twenty-three of forty-five (51 percent).

[46] High rates of participation since independence have been achieved by such microstates at Bahrain (four of five treaties, or 80 percent), Grenada (100 percent), Qatar (80 percent), and the United Arab Emirates (100 percent). Low rates have been recorded by Equatorial Guinea (two of seven treaties, or 28.6 percent), the Maldives (0.0 percent), Nauru (20 percent), Tonga (20 percent), and Western Samoa (20 percent). Recency of independence in the case of most of these microstates may distort their records, whether high or low.

[47] These forty-one include the four with 100 percent records (p. 80) and seven with near-perfect records (95 percent to 99 percent)—Australia, Brazil, Canada, Egypt, Greece, the Netherlands, and Norway.

better attendance records, including five with 100 percent participation since they achieved independence.[48] To summarize, seventy-five countries—or 48.4 percent of the total—have participated in 70 percent or more of the multipartite international conferences they could have attended.[49] On the other end of the spectrum, twenty-two states (14.2 percent) participated at a rate of less than 40 percent of possible conference attendance.[50] The remaining fifty-eight countries (37.4 percent) averaged from 40 percent to 70 percent of possible conference attendance.

The overall actual conference participation ratio is high, therefore, in relation to attendance potential, determined in the case of each state on the basis of the date of its independence, as illustrated by the following summary tabulation:

Attendance in Relation to Potential (percent)	Number of States	Attendance in Relation to Potential (percent)	Number of States
100	11	40-49	12
90-99	18	30-39	2
80-89	28	20-29	7
70-79	18	10-19	1
60-69	23	1- 9	3
50-59	23	0	9

Since conference participation may depend not only on the interests and willingness of the individual country, but also on conference initiation, purpose, and invitation, these latter factors need to be examined in order to assess developments and trends. For example, attendance at the eight conclaves between 1943 and 1946 to draft the constitutions of the United Nations and other multipartite agencies was generally prohibited to the Axis powers, and some of these conferences were closed to wartime neutrals. Thirty-one of the pre-World War II powers attended all of these conferences, as did India, but Germany and Japan were not invited to any of them. Axis-occupied or affiliated states—such as Albania, Austria, Bulgaria, Finland, Hungary, Italy, Romania, and Thailand—also were largely

[48] Bangladesh, Kenya, Mauritius, Swaziland, and Uganda.

[49] This includes eleven with 100 percent records and another sixty-four with better than 70 percent attendance.

[50] Of these, nine countries have completely abstained to date, but, as noted, six of these are new states that have not had sufficient opportunity to establish patterns of involvement.

excluded,[51] as were Portugal and Spain and such neutrals as Ireland, Sweden, and Switzerland. A few countries, including Afghanistan, Mongolia, Saudi Arabia, Vatican City, and the Yemen Arab Republic (San'a) also had low participation rates, but for other reasons. Germany and Mongolia are the only prewar states that were not a party to any of the fifteen constitutive conferences, whereas some of the states excluded from those convened during World War II became more active after 1946.

As another illustration of modest participation levels resulting from limited invitation, only twenty-one of the wartime United Nations were represented at the Paris conference to sign the European Axis satellite peace treaties in 1946. Although fifty-two attended the San Francisco conference in 1951 at which the Japanese peace treaty was signed, China, India, Thailand, and the European Axis and neutral powers did not. No microstate attended either of these peace-making conclaves.

On the other hand, conferences called by the United Nations organization usually are universal, with invitations normally issued to all of its members, and often to nonmembers as well.[52] For this reason, and because large-scale multipartite conferences are being increasingly initiated by the United Nations and its specialized agencies to deal with broad issues of policy formulation and rule making, involvement in such conferences tends to become inclusive. As the membership of these international institutions grows, the quantity of conference participation is bound to increase.

Table 10 presents participation figures, according to population categories, for each of the forty-five international conferences under review. The fifteen constitutive conferences, convened between 1943 and 1956, appear in chronological sequence in the upper part of the

---

[51] Poland is an exception. It attended all of the early conferences except the United Nations Charter negotiations at San Francisco in 1945, as discussed in Chapter 6. Although occupied by Axis powers, some countries that had governments in exile, such as Denmark, Greece, the Netherlands, Norway, and Yugoslavia, managed to attend nearly all of the constitutive conferences.

[52] Increasingly, when the United Nations and its specialized agencies sponsor ad hoc international conferences, they invite national liberation movements and other international organizations to send observership missions. For example, in 1974, under a U.N. resolution, Papua New Guinea (not yet independent) and all liberation movements recognized by the Organization of African Unity and the Arab League were invited to send delegations to the world population conference. Six African, Mideast, and Seychelle Islands liberation groups attended the world food conference as observers. The Cook Islands, the Netherlands Antilles, Papua New Guinea, and the United States Trust Territory of the Pacific sent observer delegations to the law of the sea conference at Geneva in 1975.

table. Attendance at these ranged from thirty-six to eighty-four states. Except where deliberate political exclusion pertained, variations seem to be due largely to newness, smallness, and functional selectivity. Before 1946—except for one gathering, the Chicago civil aviation conference—participation ranged between forty-four and fifty states, with the largest number of governments (but including no microstate) represented at San Francisco to sign the United Nations Charter in 1945. The following year, sixty-one national delegations convened in New York to create the World Health Organization. Two later conferences—concerned with the General Agreement on Tariffs and Trade (GATT) at Geneva in 1947 and with establishing the Intergovernmental Maritime Consultative Organization at Geneva the following year—attracted forty or fewer states, whereas those concerned with telecommunication and postal affairs (respectively at Atlantic City in 1947 and Brussels in 1952) and with creating the International Atomic Energy Agency at New York in 1956 were attended by seventy-eight to eighty-four. More revealing, however— excluding the Axis powers and Europe's World War II neutrals[53]— 82 percent of the then independent states attended the San Francisco Conference in 1945. Even higher participation ratios were achieved by some of the later constitutive conferences.[54] No microstates were present at six of these fifteen constitutive gatherings, only one appeared at seven of them, and two attended the sessions on the telecommunication and postal unions.

For the remaining thirty international conferences held between 1946 and 1975, one may observe a chronological increase in participation, due in part to the growth of the number of independent countries. Before 1960, only a few of the meetings attracted more than sixty governments, and the exceptions dealt with such popular matters as radio regulations, the protection of war victims, and the peaceful uses of atomic energy.[55] It was at the law of the sea conferences in the late 1950s that attendance began to mount significantly.[56] During

---

[53] Eight Axis powers, three neutrals, Poland, Portugal, and Spain.

[54] Attendance relative to post-independence potentiality was 91.3 percent for the Universal Postal Union conference at Brussels in 1952 and 88 percent for the International Atomic Energy Agency conference at New York in 1956. By comparison, attendance was only 45.6 percent at the Intergovernmental Maritime Consultative Organization conference at Geneva in 1948, and 51.3 percent at the meeting the preceding year to negotiate the General Agreement on Tariffs and Trade.

[55] Radio, Atlantic City (1947)—seventy-eight states; war victims, Geneva (1949)— sixty-one states; and atomic energy, Geneva (1955)—seventy-one states.

[56] Geneva (1958)—eighty-five states, and London (1959)—eighty-six states.

Table 10

MULTIPARTITE INTERNATIONAL CONFERENCE PARTICIPATION, BY POPULATION CATEGORY

International Conferences	Participation (number of states)										
	A (5)	B (11)	C (16)	D (47)	E (50)	F (13)	G (6)	H (1)	I (2)	J (4)	Total (155)
Constitutive Conferences [a]											
UNRRA,[b] Atlantic City, 1943	0	1	1	14	18	9	1	1	0	3	48
International Bank and Monetary Fund, Bretton Woods, 1944	0	1	1	13	17	7	1	1	0	3	44
ICAO, Chicago, 1944	0	1	1	16	22	10	1	1	0	2	54
United Nations, San Francisco, 1945	0	0	1	15	21	8	1	1	0	3	50
FAO, Quebec, 1945	0	1	1	13	20	6	1	1	0	3	46
UNESCO, London, 1945	0	0	1	12	20	7	1	1	0	2	44
WHO, New York, 1946	0	0	1	19	25	10	2	1	0	3	61
ILO, Montreal, 1946	0	1	1	11	22	6	2	1	0	2	46
GATT, Geneva, 1947	0	0	1	5	21	8	2	1	0	2	40
ITU, Atlantic City, 1947	1	1	2	22	31	12	3	1	2	3	78
WMO, Washington, D.C., 1947	0	1	2	19	26	8	3	1	1	3	64
ITO,[c] Havana, 1947/1948	0	0	1	16	24	8	3	1	1	2	56
IMCO, Geneva, 1948	0	0	0	8	17	5	3	1	0	2	36
UPU, Brussels, 1952	1	1	2	23	35	13	3	1	2	3	84
IAEA, New York, 1956	0	1	1	23	35	12	3	1	2	3	81

Table 10 (continued)

International Conferences	Participation (number of states)										
	A (5)	B (11)	C (16)	D (47)	E (50)	F (13)	G (6)	H (1)	I (2)	J (4)	Total (155)
Others (Post-World War II)											
European Axis Peace Treaties, Paris, 1946	0	0	0	2	10	4	1	1	0	3	21
Radio Regulations, Atlantic City, 1947	1	1	1	23	33	10	3	1	2	3	78
Freedom of Information,d Geneva, 1948	0	0	1	14	26	9	3	1	0	3	57
Safety of Life at Sea, London, 1948	0	1	0	6	14	6	3	1	0	3	34
Protection of War Victims, Geneva, 1949	1	0	1	14	26	11	3	1	1	3	61
Japanese Peace Treaty, San Francisco, 1951	0	0	1	15	21	8	2	1	2	2	52
Copyright, Geneva, 1952	1	0	1	12	18	7	3	1	2	2	47
Opium (Narcotics Control),d New York, 1953	0	0	0	7	14	10	4	0	2	2	39
Protection of Cultural Property in Armed Conflict, The Hague, 1954	1	0	1	10	23	9	3	1	2	3	53
Pollution of Sea by Oil, London, 1954	0	0	0	11	15	7	4	1	1	3	42
Conservation of Resources of Sea,d Rome, 1955	0	1	0	12	20	8	3	1	2	3	50
Peaceful Uses of Atomic Energy,d Geneva, 1955	1	1	1	16	29	13	4	1	2	3	71
Air—Amending Warsaw Convention, The Hague, 1955	0	0	1	12	16	6	3	1	1	3	43
Maritime Law, Brussels, 1957	1	0	0	4	18	6	3	1	2	3	38
Law of the Sea (First),d Geneva, 1958	1	1	1	23	37	12	4	1	2	3	85

Conference											Total
International Commercial Arbitration,d New York, 1958	1	0	0	10	17	9	4	1	2	3	47
Industrial Property, Lisbon, 1958	1	0	1	10	22	6	3	1	2	2	48
Law of the Sea (Second),d London, 1959	1	1	1	24	36	13	4	1	2	3	86
Safety of Life at Sea, London, 1960	0	1	1	10	23	11	3	1	2	3	55
Diplomatic Relations,d Vienna, 1961	1	0	1	20	34	13	5	1	2	3	80
Application of Science and Technology for Benefit of Less Developed Countries,d Geneva, 1963	1	0	4	28	41	11	5	1	2	3	96
Consular Relations,d Vienna, 1963	1	0	2	30	37	13	4	1	2	3	93
Trade and Development,d Geneva, 1964	1	1	5	40	44	13	5	1	2	3	115
Human Rights,d Tehran, 1968	1	0	3	19	38	14	3	1	2	3	84
Peaceful Uses of Outer Space,d Vienna, 1968	1	0	1	19	34	12	4	1	2	3	77
Human Environment,d Stockholm, 1972	1	3	12	35	38	10	6	1	2	2	110
World Population,d Bucharest, 1973	1	7	13	43	46	13	6	1	2	3	135
World Food, 1974	1	6	12	43	44	13	6	1	2	3	131
Law of the Sea (Third),d Geneva, 1975	3	5	11	30	32	12	4	1	2	4	104
International Women's Year,d Mexico City, 1975	2	6	13	41	44	12	6	1	2	4	131
Total	26	44	106	812	1,204	430	144	44	59	126	2,995
Percent of total participation	0.9	1.5	3.5	27.1	40.2	14.3	4.8	1.5	2.0	4.2	100.0

a For key to abbreviations of organizations, see p. 97.
b United Nations Relief and Rehabilitation Administration (now defunct).
c International Trade Organization (never activated).
d Indicates conferences called by the United Nations.
Source: See source for Appendix A.

this period, conferences initiated by the United Nations or its specialized agencies generally but not always drew substantial attendance.[57]

All of the conferences since 1960 considered in this analysis were initiated by the United Nations, and attendance ranged from 77 to 135,[58] with six of the last eight attracting more than 100 participating states. Microstates were unrepresented at six of the twenty-five conferences before 1970 and only one or two microstates were present at the other nineteen; however, an average of seven have participated in the five most recent gatherings.

Despite a trend toward universalizing invitations and expanding conference participation, several countries continue their minimal involvement in nonconstitutive as well as constitutive conferences. These include certain of the microstates and Communist countries. Microstates not affiliated with the United Nations—like Nauru and Tonga—have attended only one or two of these conferences since they gained independence, as was also the case with Western Samoa, which joined the United Nations in 1976.[59] Other microstates that are U.N. members—the Bahamas, Bahrain, Barbados, Qatar, and the United Arab Emirates—have attended from two to five conferences sponsored by the United Nations since 1972.

The Communist countries most guilty of minimum participation are the People's Republic of China, the Democratic Republic of Germany, the Democratic People's Republic of Korea, the Democratic Republic of Vietnam, and Mongolia. The first four represent divided countries, and the differentials between their Communist and democratic components is dramatic. The participation ratio of Communist China, East Germany, North Korea, and North Vietnam has been negligible, ranging from approximately 5 percent to 15 percent of potential. In comparison, attendance by their democratic counterparts—Nationalist China, West Germany, South Korea, and South Vietnam—has ranged from 61 to 90 percent. Whether East Germany will become more active now that it has been admitted to U.N. membership, and whether North Korea, the combined Socialist Republic of Vietnam, and Mongolia will continue their voluntary isolation remains to be seen. In recent years the political division of the

---

[57] Exceptions were the New York opium/narcotics control conference in 1953—only thirty-nine states, and the international commercial arbitration conference at New York five years later—forty-seven states.

[58] The Vienna conference on the peaceful uses of outer space in 1968—77 states, and the world population conference at Bucharest in 1973—135 states.

[59] All three attended the 1975 conference on the law of the sea, but the Maldives, although a U.N. member and an insular state, did not. The same is true of the two 1976 sessions of the conference.

countries appears to have ceased to constitute an automatic restraint on the dual participation of the two Germanies and the two Koreas, and with the defeat of South Vietnam by North Vietnam, the latter, which previously preferred noninvolvement, may change its policy.

The situation respecting China differs substantially from other divided countries. The Republic of China was an active participant (with a record of better than 83 percent of potential) to 1973, while the People's Republic of China abstained completely from participation. The latter was seated as a member of the United Nations in 1971, was subsequently invited to join in United Nations-sponsored conferences, and has attended regularly since 1973. At the same time Nationalist China withdrew from participation, so that the People's Republic appears to be replacing it. The Taipei government is being by-passed except for those conferences that are initiated by international organizations in which it still retains membership and a few ad hoc conferences convened by friendly governments. As in the past, it appears unlikely that the two Chinas will attend the same international gathering.[60]

Some comment is needed about the relation of the functional interests of states and their conference participation. Of the thirty nonconstitutive conferences, those convened to deal with the World War II peace treaties for obvious reasons achieved relatively low participation levels, but certain other conferences, such as those concerned with maritime affairs, commercial aviation, and economic controls (including copyright, trademarks, the protection of cultural property, and commercial arbitration) were also, for reasons less clear, sparsely attended. Conversely, it is not difficult to understand why those conferences that dealt with diplomatic and consular relations, radio communications, and the application of science and technology for the benefit of the less-developed countries attracted extensive interest.

The most widely attended international conferences have been the recent United Nations-promoted global conclaves on such fundamental issues of common interest as trade and development, the law

---

[60] Another peculiarity worthy of note is a recent change in South Africa's international conference attendance record. Fairly constant in participation until 1972 (maintaining a rate of 83 percent of potential for thirty years), it has been obliged to discontinue attending the conferences. This grew out of its suspension by the General Assembly of the United Nations in 1974, when, as a credentials consideration, South Africa was denied the right to participate in the Assembly even though it was not expelled from the United Nations. As a consequence, it is being excluded from international conferences called by the General Assembly and its subagencies. Although it attended the early sessions of the law of the sea conference in 1958 and 1959, it was not in attendance at subsequent sessions held in 1975 and 1976.

of the sea, the human environment, population expansion, the food problem, and women's rights—all of which were attended by delegations representing more than 100 countries.[61] Notwithstanding factors of size, international organization membership and sponsorship, cost, and national prestige, the participation of some states continues to reflect discretion based on functional interest and anticipated benefits. And it seems only logical that such discretion is more likely to be decisive in the policy decisions of smaller and poorer countries, especially the microstates.

On the other hand, in view of the potential expansion of the community of nations to 200 or more, the number of microstates participating in international conferences could also mushroom, unless current trends toward wholesale inclusion are restrained or reversed. Instead of fifty parties to the negotiation of the United Nations Charter, or the hundred-plus levels at recent conferences, it is not inconceivable that important future treaty-making conclaves may involve so many national missions, so many delegates, so many position papers and commentaries, so much discussion, and so many votes in committees and plenary meetings that both the process and the end-products will be hindered if not smothered. It is not capricious to ask whether some of the recent massive forums have not produced more facade than substance, and whether some that deal with critical legal and political matters are not more delayed and frustrated than they ought to be. Nor is it unreasonable to wonder whether the international community, facing large-scale proliferation and enmeshed by a momentum of extending involvement for the sake of universality—or universality for the sake of involvement—is not approaching the threshold of self-induced sterility.

Policy Issues

In addition to such factors as the political attitude of individual states toward involvement, selectivity of partners and functions, promotion of national interests, and recency of independence, size appears to have a direct and critical bearing on participation in bilateral treaty making with the United States, major multilateral treaty relations, and international conference attendance. Collectively, microstates are among the least active, appearing at or near the bottom of the scale and accounting for less than 5 percent of participation in these

---

[61] From 1958 to 1976 the number of states attending the law of the sea conferences increased progressively from 85 to approximately 150—the largest conference size to date.

three fields of diplomatic practice. This generalization applies to both actual and potential attendance at international conferences. Interestingly, microstates rate highest in their involvement in multilateral treaties and lowest in conference participation. As a group, they tend to be more restrictive or selective than more populous states about the functional subjects of the treaties they ratify and the conferences they attend. A few microstates, like Iceland, are relatively cooperative in both treaty making and conferencing, some establish moderate or high rates of involvement with one or another of the international activities but low rates with respect to the rest, and still others remain minimal participants in all of them.

A number of recognizable peculiarities characterize the involvement of microstates—and other specific groups as well—in both treaty-making and international conferences. For example, influences on the bilateral treaty relations of other countries with the United States include geographic location, geographic proximity, economic and political affinity, alliance commitments, historical association, and source of the initiative. Insular status and recency of independence affect the extent of microstates' ratification of multipartite treaties, but location and past relationship with the United States are less pertinent than in the case of bilateral agreements. The degree of microstate engagement in international conferences entails such special factors as inclusion or exclusion by sponsoring governments and agencies, the substantial cost of widespread and possibly lengthy representation, the prestige that may accrue from conferring with larger powers, as legal equals, around the negotiating table, and possibly membership in the United Nations and other global international organizations—all of which are less material to the treaty process.

Among the principal concerns of the microstates in treaty-making and international conferences are their fundamental perceptions of involvement and responsibility, their capacity to assume the obligations that result, and the benefits they expect to derive. Each microstate will decide these matters in keeping with its own interests and resources, but the extent of its participation is bound to reflect not only its willingness but also its ability to function effectively as a normal and active member of the family of nations.

The microstates' natural limitations raise the issue whether the international community should tolerate an increasing number of low-level participants and nonparticipants. Specifically, one may well wonder whether microstates should have as much discretion as larger powers to subscribe to multipartite law-creating treaties like those that deal with the rules of war, diplomatic representation and consular arrangements, copyright and trademark protection, and jurisdiction over the continental shelf and territorial seas, as well as those devoted to the peaceful settlement of disputes—in most of which, in the past, they have evidenced little interest. In other words, are microstates to be permitted, or invited, to enjoy the benefits of advantageous treaties without also shouldering the responsibilities?

The members of the international community may need to examine whether microstates, simply because they are independent, should be encouraged to join freely in major worldwide conclaves; what they can contribute to the aggregate community and its practical functioning; and whether conference business can be handled more effectively and advantageously by restricting participation to the more globally and regionally responsible states. Because treaty making and negotiation at the conference table are vital to the orderly conduct of international affairs, a central issue for the world community is whether micro- and other small states are assets or encumbrances to these fundamental forums and processes, and whether, in the event of substantial proliferation and participation of microstates, the conduct of global and intergovernmental affairs will be enhanced or impeded.

6
INTERNATIONAL
ORGANIZATIONS

Theoretically, independent statehood presumes qualification to become a member of the United Nations and other international organizations, and to participate as a legal equal in such continuing diplomatic forums.[1] The microstates' qualifications and capabilities in this regard have evoked interest and comment, and no few misgivings, especially in view of potential proliferation.

Even though independence opens the gates to statehood and legal status in the family of nations, membership in international organizations is by no means automatic. Each individual country has the option of deciding for itself with which agencies it wishes to affiliate. If the state elects to join an existing agency, it must be authorized by the organization to do so, and usually it needs to be admitted by its members according to prescribed procedures. To became an original member of a nascent organization, the state must participate in the framing of its constitutive treaty or agreement, which it must ratify or otherwise accede to.

Universality versus Restricted Participation

The principle of universality generally pervades the issue of membership in the United Nations, its specialized agencies, and many other global and regional multipartite international organizations. When the League of Nations was created after World War I, it was intended

---

[1] The concept of international organization used in this chapter is restricted to public institutions in the traditional sense, and it is not meant to include nongovernmental organizations, multinational corporations, and similar participants in world affairs. Attention is paid primarily to multipartite organizations, although bipartite agencies are not precluded.

to become the forum of all "fully self-governing" states, dominions, and colonies that were deemed to be acceptable to its members.[2] On the other hand, the founders of the U.N. organization originally conceived it as being restricted to the World War II allies,[3] with other states, including the wartime neutrals, to be admitted only at the discretion of its members. Subsequently it was converted into a universal organization—in both principle and practice—as were its specialized agencies and the International Court of Justice.

Not possessing broad political functions, but concerned with promoting collaboration in developmental, service, and assistance programs, the specialized agencies, some of which antedate the United Nations, might well be considered even more likely prospects for universal participation. Much the same may be said of other functionally oriented global organizations not affiliated with the United Nations. Such organizations are usually open to the membership of all qualifying and interested states, including microstates.

Regional organizations are restricted to states that meet specified geographic qualifications. Important regional institutions have been created in Africa, Asia, Europe, the Mideast, and the Western Hemisphere. Some of these organizations, such as the regional banks and development associations, also admit selected outside states. The spirit of universality also influences regional groups so that they aspire to comprehensive participation within their geographic areas and, at present, place no bar to affiliation and membership on grounds of size.

In 1945 the Department of State reported that during the preceding decade the United States had been a member of approximately 320 public international organizations—216 multipartite and 104 bipartite. Many of these were temporary wartime agencies, and some had already been either terminated or superseded.[4] Several years

---

2 League of Nations Covenant, Article 1, paragraph 2.

3 Participation in the San Francisco Conference of 1945 was limited to the wartime United Nations, attested to by the signing of the United Nations Declaration and by the participants' declaration of war upon at least one of the Axis powers by March 1, 1945. Only three states that did not meet these requirements—Argentina, Byelorussia, and the Ukraine—were invited to participate, and these only at the last moment. One other nation—Poland—although not invited to San Francisco because of disagreement between East and West concerning its government, became an original member of the United Nations. For commentary, see U.S. Department of State, *Postwar Foreign Policy Preparation, 1939-1945* (Washington, D.C.: Government Printing Office, Department of State Publication 3580, 1949), pp. 377, 385, 392-393, 396, and 410. Also see United Nations Charter, Article 3.

4 U.S. Department of State, *International Agencies in Which the United States Participates* (Washington, D.C.: Government Printing Office, Department of State Publication 2699, 1946).

later, the department identified sixty-six multipartite organizations with which the United States was affiliated and thirty-three that had become defunct. The active agencies varied from the United Nations (then with fifty-nine members) and its specialized agencies to the South Pacific Commission (six members), the Council of Foreign Ministers (five members), the Caribbean Commission (four members), and several tripartite commissions.[5] Currently there are some 225 to 250 multipartite and bipartite official intergovernmental organizations, and states have the opportunity to affiliate with a broad range of permanent diplomatic institutions. The United States, for example, is a member of approximately 75 multipartite agencies, including the United Nations, the International Court of Justice, 15 U.N. specialized agencies, more than 20 additional global organizations, at least half a dozen regional banks and related financial institutions, approximately 10 inter-American and as many other regional organizations, and various commodity and other agencies.

Affiliation with international organizations possesses innate and positive appeal to states regardless of their population or territorial size, although obviously individual states will differ greatly in determining which they join. Presumably all governments harbor some desire to participate and value a sense of belonging, seek a voice and vote in collective discussion and decision making, and promote the enhancement of their national prestige. However, the older, larger, and more established powers generally take these factors for granted, or at least in stride, and display little conscious or articulated concern with them, whereas smaller and newer states, believing they are under greater compulsion to prove themselves and justify their status, to themselves as well as to others, often pay them great attention.

States join international organizations for the advantages they expect to derive from them—ranging from the management of aggression and geopolitical stabilization to the more obvious and pragmatic regulation of specific national and international activities and a broad spectrum of agricultural, cultural, health, developmental, and other forms of assistance. It would appear, however, that the newer and smaller countries have more material advantage to gain—particularly in comparison with their capacity to contribute—in services, technology, and economic aid. As a consequence, they are prone to join as many international organizations as possible that deal with matters affecting their national interests and do not impinge too severely on their birth-

[5] U.S. Department of State, *International Organizations in Which the United States Participates, 1949* (Washington, D.C.: Government Printing Office, Department of State Publication 3655, 1950).

right, that is, organizations in which the advantages exceed the costs in terms of both financial contributions and the burden of other responsibilities.

It is no surprise, therefore, that small states—including the microstates—tend to join more eagerly and participate more actively in international organizations than they do in some of the other diplomatic processes and forums. Their ability to fulfill their share of responsibilities in certain organizations may, nevertheless, be seriously questioned. The older and larger powers have allowed the problem of membership proliferation to intensify in most international organizations simply by not controlling it. A few, such as the financial agencies, reflect an awareness of the issue by equating voting with contribution through a weighted decision-making process. The United Nations Charter specifies that membership is open to "peace-loving states" that accept the commitments of the Charter and *"in the judgment of the Organization, are able and willing"* to carry them out,[6] but the United Nations has failed to define and apply these prescriptions as they relate to diminutive applicants.

Among the primary responsibilities of an international organization's members are advance preparation for and thoughtful engagement in the deliberative and negotiating processes of its councils as well as its committees (not merely voting in its plenary sessions), providing financial support, and participating in its collective defense and peace-keeping functions where needed. Both the willingness and ability of the member state to fulfill these responsibilities are crucial membership qualifications. The central issues of microstate involvement are how much membership proliferation can and should be tolerated by the global community, to what extent the majority of smaller states is to determine policy and procedure for the minority of larger powers, and how wide the gulf may grow between cost and benefit, between power wielding and community interest, and between votes and responsibility.

United Nations and Other Global Organizations

Membership of microstates and other countries in twenty contemporary global international organizations has been reviewed for this analysis. The organizations include the seventeen components of the U.N. system and three other independent agencies of general appeal.

---

[6] United Nations Charter, Article 4; emphasis added.

Following are the names of these organizations, with the number of member nations:

United Nations System
    General
        United Nations (UN)—144
        International Court of Justice (ICJ)—145
    Specialized Agencies—Financial
        International Bank (IB)—125
        International Development Association (IDA)—113
        International Finance Corporation (IFC)—100
        International Monetary Fund (IMF)—126
    Specialized Agencies—Others
        Food and Agriculture Organization (FAO)—131
        Intergovernmental Maritime Consultative Organization (IMCO)—87
        International Atomic Energy Agency (IAEA)*—105
        International Civil Aviation Organization (ICAO)—129
        International Labor Organization (ILO)—125
        International Telecommunication Union (ITU)—140
        United Nations Educational, Scientific and Cultural Organization (UNESCO)—131
        Universal Postal Union (UPU)—144
        World Health Organization (WHO)—140
        World Intellectual Property Organization (WIPO)—70
        World Meteorological Organization (WMO)—132
Other International Organizations
    General Agreement on Tariffs and Trade (GATT)—94
    International Union for the Publication of Customs Tariffs (IUPCT)—78
    Permanent Court of Arbitration (PCA)—71

    * The International Atomic Energy Agency is not, strictly speaking, a specialized agency, but is generally regarded as part of the United Nations system.

When the United Nations was established in 1945, it consisted of fifty-one World War II anti-Axis allies and associated states,[7] and at its first session the following year, four additional countries were added,[8] raising the total to fifty-five. In thirty years, its membership nearly tripled to 144 states, and three additional members were ad-

---

[7] Including Argentina, Byelorussia, and the Ukraine (see footnote 3).

[8] These were Afghanistan, Iceland, Siam/Thailand, and Sweden.

mitted in 1976, enlarging it to 147. Because participants in the United Nations automatically become parties to the statute of the International Court of Justice,[9] they are also members of that world tribunal. However, states may join the latter without affiliating with the United Nations, which Switzerland and two European principalities elected to do, so that the court has 150 participating members.[10]

Not only are both of these institutions universalistic in spirit, they also are virtually universal in practice. By January 1976 only eleven independent countries had failed to join the United Nations. Four of these were microstates;[11] they were not excluded, but rather elected not to exercise the option of applying for membership.[12] The other twelve microstates (including four that gained independence in 1974 and 1975) became members.[13]

In 1946 the United Nations had only four members (8 percent) whose population numbered less than 5 million, and of these Iceland was the only microstate.[14] Currently, while all of the thirteen large states (population categories G to J) and fifty-six of the medium-sized countries (categories E and F) belong to the United Nations, more than half of its members (52 percent) are under 5 million, and twenty-eight (19 percent) fall below 1 million. This means that one of every five delegates to the General Assembly represents less population than the metropolitan area of Portland, Oregon. Twelve U.N. members (8 percent) are microstates, so that one of every twelve delegates represents less than 300,000 people.

On the basis of past practice, if the remaining microstates apply for membership in the United Nations and the International Court,

---

[9] United Nations Charter, Article 93.

[10] The two European principalities are Liechtenstein and San Marino. Analysis in this chapter, however, because it relates to independent countries, is based on a membership figure of 145 for the court as of January 1976.

[11] Nauru, Tonga, Vatican City, and Western Samoa; however, Western Samoa applied and was admitted in 1976.

[12] The other states that had not joined the United Nations by January 1976 were Switzerland (which had not applied for membership), Angola (which gained independence late in 1975 and became involved in civil strife), and five states whose admission to membership involved serious political considerations, including the Republic of China, the two Koreas, and the two Vietnams (later combined). The Seychelles and Transkei became independent in 1976, and Angola and the Seychelles were admitted to U.N. membership in 1976.

[13] The Bahamas, Bahrain, Barbados, Cape Verde Islands, Comoro Islands, Equatorial Guinea, Grenada, Iceland, the Maldives, Qatar, São Tomé and Príncipe, and the United Arab Emirates. As noted, the Seychelles and Western Samoa were added in 1976.

[14] U.S. Department of State, Gist, January 1974. The others were Costa Rica, Luxembourg, and Panama. Luxembourg's population remains under half a million.

they are not likely to be turned down, assuming that there is no great political opposition to their admission. It appears that size is no obstacle to participation. If this condition continues, it is axiomatic that the United Nations and the court will become almost as large as the community of nations, and will expand as rapidly as new nations proliferate.

Perhaps basing its projection on U.N. consideration of future candidates for self-determination and independence,[15] the Department of State postulates the possibility of expansion to approximately 200 members in a few years. Not only would this mean quadrupling the original membership, but, because fifty of the new members would have populations of less than 100,000, roughly one of every four participants would be a submicrostate.

This could change materially the composition and functioning of the United Nations. Small states (under 5 million in population) would wield nearly two-thirds of the voting power and could dominate the international forum. If all the territories projected in Chapter 3 were to gain independence and join, the United Nations would consist of nearly 300 members, with small states controlling three-fourths of its votes, smaller states (under 1 million) exercising a majority of the voting power, and microstates commanding two of every five votes.[16]

In the overall U.N. system—composed of the fifteen specialized agencies as well as of the United Nations and the International Court—several important developments may be noted. Summary comparative membership statistics are presented in Table 11. Except for the Universal Postal Union (144 members), the International Telecommunication Union (140), and the World Health Organization (140), membership drops below the participation standard of the United Nations and the court. The Intergovernmental Maritime Consultative Organization (87 members), the World Intellectual Property Organization (70 members), and the financial institutions (ranging from 126 down to 100 members) represent the less popular agencies. The overall affiliation level for the U.N. system is 79 percent—with ratios varying from more than 90 percent of the world's nations in the United Nations and the World Court to 75 percent in the International Bank together with the other financial agencies. The 155 independent states on average participate in more than thirteen of the seventeen organizations.

---

[15] See pp. 27-28.

[16] Computations for the last two categories exclude the twenty-five unpopulated entities listed in Appendix B.

Table 11

INTERNATIONAL ORGANIZATION MEMBERSHIP, SUMMARY BY POPULATION CATEGORY

	Population Category (number of states)										Total (155)	Per-cent
	A (5)	B (11)	C (16)	D (47)	E (50)	F (13)	G (6)	H (1)	I (2)	J (4)		
Global												
United Nations	2	10	16	47	44	12	6	1	2	4	144	93
International Court of Justice	2	10	16	47	45	12	6	1	2	4	145	94
Financial specialized agencies (4)[a]	0	21	50	156	150	44	23	4	8	8	464	75
Other U.N. specialized agencies (11)[b]	8	55	114	424	469	133	63	11	22	35	1,334	78
GATT	1	5	13	29	28	7	6	1	2	2	94	61
Other global organizations (2)	0	2	6	40	63	19	8	2	3	6	149	48
Total	13	103	215	743	799	227	112	20	39	59	2,330	75
Percent of possibilities	13	47	67	79	80	87	93	100	98	74	75	75
Regional[c]												
General (4)	0	6	12	40	30	5	4	1	0	1	99	83
Financial (5)	0	4	7	45	40	10	8	1	2	2	119	82
Total	0	10	19	85	70	15	12	2	2	3	218	82
Percent of possibilities	0	77	59	97	85	83	92	100	100	75	82	

[a] International Bank, International Development Association, International Finance Corporation, and International Monetary Fund.
[b] For list, see p. 97.
[c] For list, see p. 103.
Source: Global organizations—compiled from Appendix A; regional organizations—computed from Union of International Organizations, *Yearbook of International Organizations* (Brussels: Union of International Organizations, 1974), as updated.

The microstates fall significantly below these norms. They maintain only a 40 percent overall participation ratio, and individually they are members of an average of less than seven of the organizations. Iceland has joined sixteen of them, and three other states—Barbados, Qatar, and the United Arab Emirates—exhibit high affiliation records; aside from the recently independent microstates,[17] the less enthusiastic participants include Nauru, Tonga, and Vatican City.[18] It appears, therefore, that despite their relative enthusiasm to join the United Nations, microstates become more selective about membership in its specialized agencies.

The financial agencies—the International Bank, International Development Association, International Finance Corporation, and International Monetary Fund—presumably would be of special value to new and less endowed states, but fail to attract high participation. The largest group of states to disdain membership in them consists of the Communist powers.[19] Only half of the microstates have joined the fund and the bank.[20] Of the remainder, four are too new (1974–1975) to determine their participation, and apparently the Maldives, Nauru, Tonga, and Vatican City choose not to apply. Except in the case of the Maldives, this parallels their record of affiliation with the United Nations and the International Court. It does not appear that smallness disbars a state from applying for, or being accepted into, membership by the global financial institutions, but in practice, even discounting the newly independent, the microstate record of participation is significantly inferior to the overall affiliation ratio, as indicated in Table 12. The microstates average membership in four of eleven of the other U.N. specialized agencies, and their preferences conform substantially with those of other states.

The United Nations and its specialized agencies appear to be by far the most attractive global international organizations, both to states in general and to the microstates. For comparative purposes, three independent agencies also are reviewed: the General Agreement on Tariffs and Trade, the International Union for the Publication of Customs Tariffs, and the Permanent Court of Arbitration. Member-

---

[17] The Cape Verde Islands, Comoro Islands, Grenada, and São Tomé and Príncipe.

[18] They are members of only two or three organizations, principally the International Telecommunication Union and the Universal Postal Union.

[19] Albania, Bulgaria, Byelorussia, the People's Republic of China, Cuba, Czechoslovakia, East Germany, Hungary, North Korea, Mongolia, Poland, the Ukraine, the Soviet Union, and Vietnam. However, Romania is a member of the bank and the fund, and Yugoslavia is affiliated with all four agencies.

[20] It is necessary to be a member of the International Monetary Fund in order to join the International Bank.

Table 12

COMPARISON OF OVERALL AND MICROSTATE PARTICIPATION IN GLOBAL INTERNATIONAL ORGANIZATIONS
(percent)

Organizations[a]	Overall Participation	Microstate Participation
United Nations	93	75
International Court of Justice	94	75
Non-financial specialized agencies (11)	78	36
Financial specialized agencies (4)	75	33
General Agreement on Tariffs and Trade	61	38
Others (2)	48	6
Overall	75	36

[a] For list of organizations, see p. 97.
Source: Computed from Table 11.

ship in these ranges from seventy-one to ninety-four. Nine micro-states have decided not to join any of them, five have affiliated with the General Agreement on Tariffs and Trade,[21] and Iceland is a member of all three. Microstate participation in other more functionally delimited global organizations, as might be anticipated, is highly selective and even more restricted.[22] Table 12 summarizes the distinction between overall and microstate participation in international organizations.

Regional Organizations

Regional intergovernmental organizations pursue universal membership in their areas, and those possessing general and financial functions enjoy widespread affiliation. As with the U.N. system, exclusion by the organizations tends to be political rather than based on standards of population size, and nonparticipation is selective on the part

[21] Barbados, Equatorial Guinea, the Maldives, Qatar, and Tonga.

[22] Following the general pattern of modest interest in such agencies as the International Hydrographic Organization (forty-one members, or 26 percent participation), the International Institute for the Unification of Private International Law (forty-eight members), the International Office of Weights and Measures (forty-three members), the Energy Coordinating Group (fourteen members), and specific commodity organizations.

of national governments.[23] The nine organizations surveyed for this analysis embrace the four general regional agencies (the Organization of American States, the Council of Europe, the League of Arab States, and the Organization of African Unity) and five financial and economic institutions (the Inter-American Development Bank, the Organization for Economic Cooperation and Development, the European Payments Union, the African Development Bank, and the Asian Development Bank).

As of 1976, all but three Western Hemisphere countries were members of the Organization of American states[24]—the Bahamas, Guyana, and Surinam—of which the Bahamas is a microstate, and all but Guyana became independent in recent years (1973–1975). Similarly, except for Finland, Portugal, Spain, and Vatican City, all non-Communist European states belong to the Council of Europe,[25] all Arab countries are affiliated with the League of Arab States,[26] and except for South Africa and Transkei (1976), which are excluded for political reasons, all continental African states are members of the Organization of African Unity.

Much the same membership pattern is evident in the regional banks and other broad-scale economic organizations. For example, among those eligible, only Cuba, Guyana, and three new states are not members of the Inter-American Development Bank,[27] and all non-Communist European countries except Cyprus and Malta have joined the Organization for Economic Cooperation and Development and the European Payments Union.[28] All but eight of the continental African powers participate in the African Development Bank,[29] and

---

[23] This analysis is based on membership statistics provided in Union of International Organizations, *Yearbook of International Organizations*, 15th ed. (Brussels: Union of International Organizations, 1974), with some updating.

[24] Canada, British Honduras (Belize), and six European states, while not full members, were admitted to observerships. Although Cuba remains a member, it has been temporarily "excluded" from participation in the Organization of American States and related agencies such as the Inter-American Defense Board.

[25] Turkey, listed as a Mideast power in this study, is also a member of the Council of Europe.

[26] Two Mideast countries—Iran and Turkey—that do not qualify as Arab states are not members of the Arab League, nor, for this and other obvious political reasons, is Israel.

[27] On the other hand, Canada is affiliated as a regular member, although it has not joined the Organization of American States and other agencies in the inter-American system.

[28] The United States and Canada also are members, and New Zealand and Yugoslavia were granted special participatory status.

[29] The exceptions include two new countries, South Africa (which is politically precluded), and five other states—the Gambia, Equatorial Guinea, Lesotho, Madagascar, and Mauritius.

membership in the Asian Development Bank embraces most Asian states located east of Iran, as well as several western Pacific powers.[30]

Consequently, it is clear that newness, occasional individual reluctance, and political objection are more important impediments to membership in regional agencies than standards of size and ability to contribute. Aside from the Communist countries and those that are otherwise deliberately precluded from membership—such as Israel and Turkey (Arab League) and South Africa (Organization of African Unity)—the overall degree of participation in these nine regional organizations is high—82 percent of the possible participants, and more than 87 percent if the new states that have scarcely had time to affiliate are exempted from consideration. These ratios, though somewhat below those of the United Nations and the International Court of Justice, nevertheless compare favorably with those of the U.N. specialized agencies, as indicated in Table 11, and they exceed substantially the level of participation in the General Agreement on Tariffs and Trade and many other global organizations.

It is also interesting to note that of the general regional organizations, the inter-American and African agencies are as universal in membership in their areas as the United Nations is globally, that the Council of Europe ranks lowest in potential membership, and that the regional financial institutions are considerably more inclusive than the International Bank, the International Monetary Fund, and their affiliates. However, in the regional agencies the membership ratio of the smaller states, under 1 million population, falls below the overall norm.[31] On the other hand, Iceland has joined all three European organizations and six other microstates are affiliated with the regional agencies.[32] If the new states (1974–1975) are excluded, Vatican City represents the sole microstate nonparticipant[33] in the regional organizations.

---

[30] Exceptions include Bangladesh, Bhutan, the Republic of China, and three Communist countries—the People's Republic of China, North Korea, and Vietnam. However, Hong Kong is included as a separate member, as are Fiji, Papua New Guinea, and Western Samoa. The United States, Canada, and twelve European countries also are members.

[31] For summary figures, see Table 11.

[32] Barbados is affiliated with the Organization of American States and the Inter-American Development Bank; Bahrain, Qatar, and the United Arab Emirates with the Arab League; Equatorial Guinea with the Organization of African Unity; and Western Samoa with the Asian Development Bank.

[33] The Maldives, Nauru, and Tonga are the only other older microstates that have not become members of such regional organizations, but they are not located within the geographic purview of these agencies. There are no separate general or financial organizations for the Pacific area.

Membership in the regional agencies would surely be affected by the emergence of numerous additional microstates. Should the proliferation envisaged in Chapter 3 occur, it is possible to foresee considerable enlargement of the Organization of American States, and some expansion of the Council of Europe and the Organization of African Unity, but little modification of the Arab League. Change in both the total membership and the relative ratio of small states would be negligible in the African and Arab agencies, and, although somewhat more substantial in the Council of Europe, it would not be revolutionary. However, the Organization of American States could double in size if the independent countries in the Western Hemisphere that have not affiliated should join, along with those territories considered for self-determination in the United Nations and a few others.[34] More than half of its members would then be microstates, and the combined population of some twenty submicrostates—composing 40 percent of its membership—would amount to less than 1 million. This could alter considerably the institutions and functioning of the inter-American system, and plans ought to be developed to cope with the potential problems.

General Policy Issues

National independence and status in the family of nations do not automatically qualify new states for, or accord them membership in, the United Nations and other international organizations. It is both practical and intellectually defensible to control organizational membership by standards other than mere nationhood. To do so would by no means predetermine the course and extent of microstate proliferation and the enlargement of the family of nations. Management of the latter would of course contribute materially in containing the possible membership explosion in the international organizations. In any case, the prospect of proliferation appears to require the development of controls, whether global, organizational, or both.

Smallness, by itself, does not preclude microstates from being admitted into membership by the United Nations and other international agencies, and, in general, small states do not differ from others in preferring those organizations of general as compared with more limited functions. While microstates, like most larger powers, tend to be joiners, they usually exercise greater selectivity toward the specialized agencies. It may be presumed that, subject to individual

---

[34] For example, French Guiana, Margarita Island, and St. Barthelemy.

exceptions, the smaller the state, the less likely it will be to diffuse its participation in a large number of global and regional international organizations, and that, as the number of small states—especially the potential submicrostates—increases, the level of nonparticipation, particularly in the more functionally restricted agencies, will increase. Microstate affiliation, however, is high in the United Nations and in those regional agencies that exercise the broadest political functions. Yet it is precisely in these organizations that the problems related to proliferation of membership by states of limited capacity to contribute are most acute, suggesting urgent consideration of the nature and feasibility of alternatives to simply continuing the unrestrained extension of membership to a host of additional microstates.

7

POLICY PROBLEMS AND OPTIONS ANALYSIS

The continuing proliferation of membership in international organizations poses many policy issues for members of the world community. Organizational, administrative, and procedural difficulties that seem minor today may become all but unmanageable when amplified by the admission of large numbers of smaller states. Financial problems are certain to intensify. These entail more than the acquisition of the resources needed to function and carry out worthy programs, which increase in price year by year and currently cost approximately $2 billion annually in the U.N. system alone. They also concern the manner of allocating assessments among members and, more significantly, relating the financial responsibility of individual members to their roles in the decision-making process. In view of recent developments, the proportionate reduction of the voting strength of the larger, more affluent states may be the most vexing of the problems.

General Operational Problems

It seems indisputable that inflated membership threatens the operational viability of international organizations. For example, the United Nations grew from the original 51 members to 99 in 1960 and 127 by 1970, and it increased by 20 in the next six years. These increases mean that currently plenary and other sessions are attended by the delegations of nearly 150 states, each of which is entitled under the Charter to appoint five delegates and five alternates as well as national missions. As elaborated in Chapter 3, if states continue to be admitted as they have in the past, the United Nations could grow to 200 members or more, conceivably even to 300. This would result in a forum of from 1,000 to 1,500 delegates, supported by an equal number of alternates and some 200 to 300 diplomatic missions. If the missions average ten staff members, the representational corps at New York would number between 4,000 and 6,000 persons.[1] Similarly, if the International Labor Organization increased to 200 members, its plenary sessions could be attended by 800 delegates, backed by their supporting staffs. (Each state is entitled to accredit four delegates—two appointed by the government, one representing management, and another representing labor.) Such mushrooming of delegations and missions is bound to slow and hinder the operation of international forums, and possibly alter their very nature.

If one uses Dean Rusk's rule of thumb that about 100 major items are considered at each regular session of the General Assembly,[2] there could be up to 14,400 votes cast in its plenary sessions alone. Projected membership expansion could raise this figure to as much as 30,000. The votes cast in General Assembly committees and special sessions, in the Security Council and other primary organs together with their committees, and in a host of subsidiary U.N. agencies might raise the number to more than 400,000. With the votes that may be cast in the plenary sessions of the eleven nonfinancial specialized agencies, computed conservatively, the potential annual number of votes in the U.N. system could reach the staggering total of 500,000. The administrative chores this would create are easy to imagine, not to mention the heavy decision-making responsibility that would accrue to smaller as well as larger states.

Every additional national delegation increases the need for space, documents, discussion, time, and operational cost. Were the United Nations to grow to 200 members, it would be obliged to expand by at least one-third, and probably more, many of its facilities and services. Years ago Inis L. Claude, Jr., reported: "The United Nations is about to run out of flagpoles, and chairs, and—unthinkable disaster!—paper. . . . The sheer numerical growth of the organization poses difficult housekeeping, procedural, and political problems." [3]

---

[1] In 1974, approximately 195 persons were assigned to the U.S. mission to the United Nations. See U.S. Department of State, *U.S. Participation in the U.N. . . . 1974* (Washington, D.C.: Government Printing Office, Department of State Publication 8827, 1975), p. 467; hereinafter reports in this series are referred to as *U.S. Participation in the U.N.*, with date.

[2] Referred to in Elmer Plischke, "The New Diplomacy: A Changing Process," *Virginia Quarterly Review*, vol. 49 (Summer 1973), p. 337. The question is raised whether more than 20 percent of such votes are based on instructions from home governments.

[3] Inis L. Claude, Jr., *The Changing United Nations* (New York: Random House, 1967), p. 62.

Membership expansion would necessitate more and larger plenary chambers, committee rooms, delegate chambers, staff offices, and related physical facilities. Document production, archives, internal and external communications networks, and other services for delegations and deliberations would have to be augmented. Many purely housekeeping functions would also be affected, including credentials certification, interpretation and translation (additional languages may be added to the official list),[4] equipment and supplies, and bookkeeping, to say nothing of the need to provide additional lounges, dining halls, personal and institutional security, parking space, and an endless list of similar matters. In general, such problems of management and administration should not be insurmountable. Nevertheless, operational efficiency could easily deteriorate with size and reach a point of diminishing returns in benefits relative to costs.

Financing

The troublesome problem of financing international organizations, experience shows, centers in the inability of the smaller states to contribute funds in proportion to their voting power as legal equals. This means in practice that the larger states must subsidize the small, not only by virtue of their financial inability or default but, increasingly, in response to organizational mandates shaped by the smaller states' disproportionate decision-making authority. Resolution of the problem appears to lie in reinterpreting the small states' status as equals. The doctrine of legal equality clearly applies to the initial determination to affiliate with an international agency and, on joining, the right to benefit from the advantages it affords. It also pertains to representation and voting, except to the extent that these may be modified by constitutive acts and internal operational rules. However, it is

---

[4] In 1973 the United Nations decided to upgrade Chinese from one of five "official" (recognized) languages to a working language and estimated that the initial annual cost of the change would exceed $1 million. At the request of nineteen Arab-speaking members, it also added Arabic as both an official and working language, on the agreement that the Arab powers bear the cost for the first three years, estimated at $8.3 million. The following year three German-speaking nations requested that selected U.N. documents be provided in German, which was approved by the General Assembly on the condition that the requesting countries pay the additional cost. See U.S. Congress, House of Representatives, *Twenty-Eighth Annual Report on U.S. Participation in the U.N., 1973* (House Document No. 93-360, 1974), p. 248 (hereinafter referred to as *U.S. Participation in the U.N., 1973*); and U.S. Department of State, *U.S. Participation in the U.N., 1974*, p. 423.

rarely applied to balance financial responsibility with membership rights.

Assessment Systems. Historically, international organizations have employed five basic assessment systems to fund their operations.[5] The simplest provides for identical contributions by all members, which has been used only by a few minimum-budget agencies,[6] and for various methods of qualified equality, also employed by a mere handful of organizations.[7] These procedures were designed to keep budgets low, to make assessments as simple as possible, and to respect the principle of equality. Realizing that higher budgets require an "ability to pay" principle, the larger international organizations have adopted alternatives similar to progressive taxation.

To establish some stratification of the ability and willingness of members to contribute financially, several of the older organizations turned to the "class system" of assessments. This usually prescribed six to eight arbitrary membership categories, with each state assigned to a specific class—often by its own choice—and each class assessed in accordance with a fixed scale. Under the 1939 Convention of the Universal Postal Union, for example, members were divided into seven categories, and a number of assessment units, ranging from one to twenty-five, were prescribed for each class. Similar systems with six classes were used by the International Telecommunication Union and the International Union for the Protection of Industrial Property.[8] The United States was invariably placed in the highest paying class in such groups. The smaller states were allowed to con-

---

[5] For analysis concerning these methods of assessment, see Plischke, *Conduct of American Diplomacy*, pp. 577-581, and for specific illustrations of assessment systems, see Plischke, *International Relations: Basic Documents*, pp. 62-64.

[6] For example, the former Central Bureau of the International Map of the World on the Millionth Scale, to which members contributed £ 10 per year. See *International Agencies in Which the United States Participates*, p. 103, and *International Organizations in Which the United States Participates*, p. 111. The latter is hereinafter referred to as *International Organizations*.

[7] The Caribbean Commission (changed to the Caribbean Organization in 1961 and disbanded four years later) used a mixed formula with one-third of the budget based on equal shares, one-third on population in the Caribbean area, and one-third on national income. See *International Organizations*, pp. 194-195. In the International Tin Study Group the members were assessed £ 500, but if this failed to provide sufficient funds, they were asked to contribute varying amounts in relation to their production or consumption of tin. See ibid., p. 66.

[8] Both the number of classes and the quantity of units assigned to each are arbitrary in this system. To compute contributions, the total number of units was divided into the budget, and the resulting unit amount was then multiplied by the number of units per class.

tribute relatively small amounts, often a twenty-fifth or a thirtieth as much as the larger powers.

The League of Nations developed another method of assessment, known as the "unit system," to refine the financial obligations of its members. Instead of grouping members by classes, a varying number of assessment units was assigned to each state. This afforded greater flexibility and discrimination than the class system.[9] In the league, assessment quotas ranged from a single unit to 105 (for the United Kingdom), in a budget totaling more than 1,000 units. The International Labor Organization and a number of agencies created during World War II also employed this unit system.[10] For a time, in the International Civil Aviation Organization the United States and the United Kingdom were assigned thirty units, and other members' quotas ranged downward to a single unit.[11] A modified and even more discriminating arrangement, used in the early days of the World Health Organization, assigned units escalating from a minimum of 5 to nearly 5,000, in a budget equivalent to more than 12,000 units; the lowest contributors thus were assessed only 0.1 percent of the highest.[12]

In order to combine a broad range of assessment variation and precise allocation among members with a simpler arithmetical process, the United Nations adopted the "percentage system" of allocations, by which each member state is assigned a specific percentage of the budget.[13] In 1946 its assessments varied from the minimum 0.04 percent to 39.89 percent for the United States.[14] From the outset, the United States contended for a contribution allotment not exceeding

---

[9] Under this arrangement, assessments were computed by dividing the total number of units into the budget, and then multiplying this amount by the number of units accorded each country.

[10] Members' quotas in the International Labor Organization ranged from 1 to 150 units (for the United States), for a total of 818 in 1949; see *International Organizations*, pp. 231-232.

[11] The United States was subsequently increased to fifty-seven units; see ibid., pp. 274-275.

[12] The United States was ascribed the largest number of units—4,787; see ibid., pp. 260-261.

[13] This system merely requires dividing the budget by each member's percentage allotment. Offsetting this simplicity of calculation is the frequent need to renegotiate the entire list of percentages, which the United Nations has been seeking to handle on a triennial cycle. Difficulty also may arise if a major contributor withdraws after an assessment schedule has been completed.

[14] See U.S. Department of State, *The United States in the United Nations . . . 1946* (Washington, D.C.: Government Printing Office, Department of State Publication 2735, 1947), pp. 124-125.

25 percent,[15] but it took more than a quarter of a century for this to be achieved (through adoption of a uniform maximum standard in the United Nations and its specialized agencies).

Most of the specialized agencies, modeling themselves after the United Nations, either adopted this percentage arrangement when established or switched to it after affiliating, so that it is now employed by nearly all of the agencies composing the U.N. system. In the process, and as a result of the uniform standard, several adjustments of the U.S. quota have been made. In those organizations to which the United States previously contributed less than a quota ranging between 25 and 33 percent of the budget—such as the Food and Agriculture and the International Civil Aviation organizations—its quota was raised, and in those agencies which used the percentage system from the outset—as in the case of the World Health Organization and UNESCO—the U.S. allotment has been reduced to 25 percent. Currently, therefore, the U.S. share of the regular budgets of the United Nations and most of its specialized agencies is fixed at 25 percent,[16] but contributions to special programs differ considerably from this norm, ranging as high as 83.4 percent for the U.N. drug abuse control program in 1973 and 84 percent for its South Asia exchange of persons program the following year. Summary budget and U.S. contribution figures, with percentages, for recent years are presented in Table 13.

To obviate certain inequities, in 1948 the United Nations adopted a "per capita ceiling" principle, under which no member state was required to contribute at a per capita rate higher than that of the state bearing the highest assessment ratio. At that time the U.S. assessment allotment, by far the highest, amounted to nearly 40 percent. It was gradually reduced, however, and as the economies of other countries flourished, their assessment rates increased. By 1974

---

[15] Senator Arthur H. Vandenberg, a delegate to the first session of the General Assembly, proposed that the United States be assessed no more than 25 percent of the budget; see U.S. Department of State, *U.S. Participation in the U.N.*, 1972, pp. 212-213.

[16] The principle of a 25 percent maximum contribution was reintroduced into the General Assembly by the United States, was adopted in 1972, and became effective in 1974. This applies only to general budgets and not to special programs based on "voluntary assessments." See ibid., pp. 212-214. However, U.S. assessments as of 1975 fell below this level in the Intergovernmental Maritime Consultative Organization (5.33 percent) and in two of the older organizations that had employed the class system of financing—the International Telecommunication Union (7.22 percent) and the Universal Postal Union (3.97 percent). In the International Atomic Energy Agency, the United States still exceeds it (27.95 percent for 1975). See U.S. Department of State, *U.S. Participation in the U.N.*, 1974, pp. 420-421.

Table 13

U.S. CONTRIBUTIONS TO UNITED NATIONS SYSTEM

(in thousands of dollars)

Budget Type	1973			1974			1975		
	Total	U.S.	Per-cent	Total	U.S.	Per-cent	Total	U.S.	Per-cent
U.N. regular budget	$ 215,279	$ 67,856	32	$ 264,322	$ 63,472	25	$ 325,075	$ 81,269	25
Specialized agencies (11 non-financial)	290,536	78,878	27	354,598	91,363	26	394,205	90,986	23
Peace-keeping operations	38,202	10,389	27	97,354	28,367	29	109,052	34,171	31
Voluntary programs	716,556	231,392	32	807,123	222,745	28	1,018,680	243,323	24
Special humanitarian programs	60,889	20,379	33	41,767	14,300	34	44,011	22,233[a]	36[a]
Total	$1,321,462	$408,894	31	$1,565,164	$420,247	27	$1,891,023	$471,982	25

[a] Apparent discrepancy is due to computing U.S. percentage only for programs to which other governments also contributed.

Source: Summarized for 1973 from U.S. Department of State, *U.S. Participation in the U.N., 1974* (Washington, D.C.: Government Printing Office, Department of State Publication 8827, 1975), pp. 432-436; for commentary respecting specific variations or complexities, see footnotes, pp. 437-438. Information for 1974 and 1975 from U.S. Department of State, *U.S. Participation in the U.N., 1975*, pp. 353-359.

several states qualified for reduced assessments under this rule, and it appeared that eight or nine would become its beneficiaries by 1977. As such states would have their contributions reduced, while those of the United States and the minimum contributors remained fixed, the difference would have to be made up by the other members falling in the median and lower per capita contribution levels. Extending this principle to the benefit of more and more members was considered to violate the more fundamental precept of capacity to pay. Acting to protect the financial status of other contributors including the smaller powers, in 1974 the General Assembly abolished the per capita ceiling principle.[17]

When the United Nations was established, the United States and the United Kingdom were burdened with half (52 percent) of the cost of financing it, while thirty-seven of the fifty-one members were assessed at rates of less than 1 percent. Of these, six contributed only 0.04 percent, which became a fixed minimum for three decades. As U.N. budgets increased and the number of smaller states multiplied, the General Assembly decided to lower this floor to 0.02 percent, effective in 1975. (This applies to regular assessments and not to the voluntary contribution programs—including certain peace-keeping operations, some of which are costly and to which smaller states often do not contribute.) This means the disparity between the highest and lowest contribution levels has increased. Small states also are assisted by an intricate "low per capita income allowance formula," under which the assessments of less developed states are reduced, and in 1972 this formula was further liberalized by the General Assembly, thereby increasing the number of minimum contributors.[18] The United States has been contributing some $400 million to $500 million annually to the United Nations and its specialized agencies in recent years, averaging more than the standard 25 percent. A microstate belonging only to the United Nations and at the minimum assessment pays about $65,000, a mere .014 percent of the contribution of the United States.

---

[17] See U.S. Department of State, *U.S. Participation in the U.N., 1974*, pp. 421-422. The per capita ceiling principle has been operative in the Organization of American States since 1949, but in this case the United States, the largest contributor, is assessed at the rate of 66 percent, which is so large that other states are not likely to increase sufficiently to require modification or elimination of the principle.

[18] This device helps to lower the assessment quota of states down to the minimum, and therefore increases the number of minimum contributors. For explanation of this intricate formula, see House of Representatives, *U.S. Participation in the U.N., 1973*, p. 249.

A fifth system of financing international organizations equates assessment and voting power. This relationship is ignored in the United Nations, most of its specialized agencies, and many regional organizations. As a consequence, each member of the United Nations, large or small, exercises equal voting rights notwithstanding that under the revised financing formula seventy-eight members (54 percent of the total) are assessed the minimum of only 0.02 percent.[19] This group includes all of the micro-members, most of the other small countries (population categories C and D), and fifteen of the medium-sized states.[20] Among the minimum contributors are such countries as Bolivia, the Congo, Ecuador, Haiti, Liberia, the Sudan, Syria, Tunisia, and Zaire. The seventy-eight members that jointly are assessed only 1.56 percent of the regular U.N. budget—one-sixteenth of the share of the United States—wield a majority of the votes in the General Assembly. Aside from being able to carry certain substantive as well as procedural issues, this enables them to determine that proposals are not "important questions" and thereby circumvent the requirement of a two-thirds vote on such matters.[21]

Moreover, the minimum contributors, supported by eighteen additional states that are assessed nominal quotas—between 0.03 percent and 0.11 percent—exercise enough votes to decide "important questions" by a two-thirds majority. Put another way, these ninety-six largely diminutive and predominantly Third World, developing countries, which jointly pay only one-fortieth of the U.N. budget, one-tenth as much as the United States, are able to dominate voting in the General Assembly.

---

[19] Sixty-three of these are small states (categories A to D) and fifteen are medium-sized, of which Ethiopia is the largest (category F).

[20] The members admitted in 1975, all of which are small states, are included in this group, which consists of the following population categories: A—two, B—ten, C—fourteen, D—thirty-seven, E—fourteen, and F—one. The twelve small states that are assessed above this minimum include five European countries (Denmark, Finland, Luxembourg, Ireland, and Norway), four Mideast and North African states (Israel, Kuwait, Lebanon, and Libya), and New Zealand, Singapore, and Uruguay. Of these, Denmark, Finland, and Norway pay the highest quotas; the others combined contribute only 1 percent of the budget. The high degree of correlation between population and financial contribution to the United Nations, especially for the micro- and other small states, is noteworthy. As additional diminutive states are admitted to membership—including the Seychelles and Western Samoa in 1976—the number and percentage of minimum contributors increases, intensifying the contribution/voting disparity.

[21] Except for those issues specified in the Charter to require a two-thirds vote. See United Nations Charter, Article 18, paragraph 2. But even some of these are subject to interpretation, determinable by vote.

The practical consequences of this imbalance are well illustrated by the General Assembly vote in 1975 that equated Zionism with racism. In this instance, a highly politicized issue was carried by a majority of only two votes (seventy-two in favor, thirty-five against, and thirty-two abstentions). Voting in favor were forty-one minimum-contribution countries, including eight microstates, whose combined financial contribution totals only 0.8 percent of the U.N. budget.[22]

In another political decision, the General Assembly passed a resolution in 1976 endorsing action by liberation movements in South Africa to seize political power "by all possible means" as well as by resort "to armed struggle," and it appealed to other states "to provide all assistance" necessary to triumph in this venture—thereby approving if not encouraging resort to force—apparently including foreign military assistance and intervention. Although the vote in favor of the resolution was substantial (108 in favor, 11 opposed, and 22 abstentions), the issue also illustrates the relationship of a voting majority to financial contributions. The favorable vote included sixty-six minimum contributors (ten of them microstates) which, combined, constituted 47 percent of the vote but provide only 1.32 percent of the U.N. assessments. All of the states voting in favor contribute less than one-third of the budget. On the other hand, the negative-voting eleven states (including the United States) subscribe to approximately 53 percent of the annual cost of the United Nations.

In recent years, small states and low contributors have determined a number of important U.N. budgetary questions, affecting the levels of financial obligations of the United States and other larger contributors. In 1973, for example, a two-year budget was adopted that increased the preceding biennial appropriation by nearly 25. percent. The Department of State objected to the magnitude of the increase and refused to support it, but the enlarged budget received the approval of a considerable majority of states, including nearly all of the low-level contributors. Jointly, the majority of 106 in this case provided less than 38 percent of the funds. The individual minimum

---

[22] Among the states that voted for the resolution, fifty are assessed at the rate of less than 1/10th of 1 percent and, combined, they contribute less than 1.4 percent, and yet they controlled 36 percent of the vote. Only six states that voted in favor of the resolution contribute more than 1 percent and, combined, their level of assessment is less than that of the United States. The contribution of all seventy-two states that voted favorably on the resolution totals 28.8 percent. The outcome would have been reversed had only one state—say, one of the Soviet Union's extra votes (Byelorussia and the Ukraine)—or one of the sub-microstates switched from favoring to abstaining or opposing the resolution. For commentary on United Nations action on the resolution, see U.S. Department of State, U.S. Participation in the U.N., 1975, pp. 212-215.

contributor had its share thereby increased by only $10,000 per year while the United States was saddled with an extra $26 million obligation for the two-year period.

In 1974 the United States sided with the minority on two important budgetary questions. One of these involved a large supplemental appropriation. The other increased the levels of U.N. salaries and allowances well beyond those of national civil service systems, a decision which, the Department of State argued, would be followed by other U.N. agencies, for which the combined initial increase would be nearly $35 million. In both instances, although the deciding majorities were substantial, the states that composed them paid less than half of the budget and of the increased appropriations. The relatively small minority of states opposing the measures were obliged to pay approximately 55 percent of the costs.

For a variety of reasons including the sheer size of the budget and the lack of economy-mindedness (while national governments were obliged to curtail expenditures), the United States in 1975 objected, in vain, to the General Assembly's approval of a substantially increased two-year budget (1976-1977). It was voted by a large majority, including most of the small contributors. The economic demands of smaller and developing countries are likely to increase, as evidenced by a recent proposal requiring that developed countries in which U.N. agencies have their headquarters pay 80 percent of the losses of such institutions resulting from inflation and currency instability.

One could certainly question whether the mini-contributors should be able to dominate decision making on budgetary matters. In effect such authority allows them to subsidize themselves or their collective interests by making levies on the treasuries of the larger states. This seems to be one of the least defensible applications of the doctrine of legal equality of sovereigns. And at least in theory there is no reason that, in financial matters, authority should not be balanced with contribution.

There are those who will contend that the present arrangement should, in fairness, be maintained because some small countries contribute to the United Nations a higher percentage of their national budgets than do the United States and other larger powers. But this is offset by the relatively greater programmatic assistance and services they derive, so that their benefits outweigh, often substantially, their costs; only if these were in balance could voting be logically equated with national budgetary quotas. In fact, relating contributions to such factors as national budgets or gross national product relative to population tends to support the argument for weighted voting. In any case, in a formula consisting of ability to pay, expected perquisites, actual and relative contribution, and voting power, the small states can scarcely be entitled to all the advantages.

Continued proliferation would produce an even greater aberration. If the rush to independence and admission to U.N. membership proceeds as it has, and the fifty sub-microstates alluded to by the Department of State were to be added to the voting roster, then nearly 150 states, the principal beneficiaries of the programs, but paying only a combined 3.5 percent of the costs, would exercise three-fourths of the voting power in the General Assembly. That this majority could and probably would use its power to increase its advantage is obvious.

Disparity between contribution and voting power is also illustrated by the functioning of the Organization of American States, in which the United States pays 66 percent of the budget but exercises only 4 percent of the voting authority. The lowest contribution levels are assigned to Grenada (0.03 percent) and Barbados (0.08 percent), and eleven other low-contributing members pay at the rate of 0.19 percent.[23] Jointly these thirteen states bear only 2.2 percent of the costs of the inter-American system but command a majority of votes. Together with three additional low-level contributors—as a group paying less than one-twentieth of the budget—these states can control two-thirds of the voting power. Conversely, the United States pays two-thirds of the budget and exercises less than one-twentieth of the voting power. This disparity would be greater if the Organization of American States were to double in size, a possibility noted in the preceding chapter. In all probability the new members would be assessed at the lowest quotas, so that the forty smaller states combined, paying less than 5 percent of the costs of the organization, would wield a dominating 83 percent of the votes.

To avoid such inequities, and reflecting the verities of international economic affairs, the equating of voting power and financial contribution has become characteristic of several commodity organizations [24] and the major post-World War II international financial

---

[23] Three other members contribute at rates below 1 percent, and only seven countries, aside from the United States, exceed this level.

[24] For example, in the International Seed Testing Association dues varied from 10 to 50 pounds sterling, corresponding to one to five votes per member. The formula for the International Sugar Council provided a scale from 1.25 percent to 21.25 percent of contribution and from one to seventeen votes. In the former Inter-American Coffee Board, the United States paid one-third of the budget and exercised one-third of the votes. See Plischke, *Conduct of American Diplomacy*, p. 579.

agencies. When the International Monetary Fund and the International Bank were created, their framers decided that each member state was to be accorded a uniform base of 250 votes plus an additional vote for each $100,000 of subscription. Under this formula the United States wielded 27,750 votes in the fund (approximately 30 percent of 92,465 votes) and 32,000 in the bank (more than 33 percent of 95,485 votes), whereas the voting strength of the smallest subscribers ranged from 252 to 260 (0.26 percent to 0.28 percent). As a result of subsequent changes in subscriptions and the extension of membership, while the number of U.S. votes has increased to between 65,000 to 70,000 in these institutions, its relative voting power has declined to less than 25 percent. Nevertheless, as an illustration of current differentials, it requires the combined votes of up to seventy-five members of the fund (61 percent) and up to eighty members of the bank (65 percent) to equal the voting strength of the United States.[25] The subsidiary agencies of the bank and the regional financial institutions utilize this same basic system for relating voting power to financial commitment.[26]

Weighted voting appears to be far better attuned to the realities of decision making in multi-million dollar financial transactions than equality of voting authority. Without it, these financial organizations probably never would have been established. It may be contended that it is unreasonable to apply the principle of voting weighted solely and arbitrarily according to financial contributions to such agencies as the United Nations and the Organization of American States. But the present system leaves much to be desired. Great disparity now exists among contributions, financial demands are burgeoning, minimum contributors continue to increase in number and their relative assessments are declining, and many high-cost programs are financed by voluntary contributions rather than as a part of regular budgets so that high contributors will pay even more and low contributors may exclude themselves from any financial obligation. At the same time, the sanctity of voting equality persists although, in actuality, the

[25] In the case of the International Monetary Fund, for example, this could include thirty-two sub-Saharan African, twenty-three Mideast and Asian, and twenty Latin American states, totaling less than 21 percent of the votes.

[26] Thus, in the International Finance Corporation voting strength varies from more than 35,000 votes for the United States (26.84 percent) and in the International Development Association from 63,750 votes for the United States (24.53 percent) to as little as 0.01 percent per country. In the Inter-American Development Bank the United States has 40 percent of the voting power, but in the Asian Development Bank it wields only 7.5 percent of the votes, and is exceeded by Japan (18 percent), Australia (8.7 percent), and India (8.7 percent), which surpass it in contributions.

voting authority of the larger states, proportionately, declines, compounding the inequity.

The issue must be posed, therefore—should not the principle of voting equality be modified? More precisely, should not the level of contribution, defined according to population and other differentials, be reflected in the decision-making process of international organizations? If so, how may this be achieved?

Possible Options

Several alternative approaches might be considered to resolve the most critical problems caused by small state proliferation in the United Nations and other international organizations. They are directed not to undoing the past, but rather toward timely and realistic action for coping with the future. They range from voluntary abstention, dissuasion, and outright exclusion to institutional and community reorganization, weighted voting, and new, more limited forms of participation.

Restricting Statehood. The most forceful way to arrest the undue expansion of international organization membership is to restrict future statehood. This would ameliorate the problems attending proliferation for both the world community and universal international agencies. However, this would require the reversal or at least the redirection of U.N. action under its self-determination policy, so it appears to be visionary and, even if widely endorsed, impractical. At best, individual states might reassess their positions and damp their automatic support of independence in favor of such alternatives as greater autonomy short of independence and more local self-rule within larger political aggregations. The latter might be more appropriate for contiguous continental areas, but may also be applicable to geographically related and culturally homogeneous insular territory.

Abstention, Dissuasion, and Exclusion. Even if independence is achieved, many small states could abstain voluntarily from joining international agencies, as in the case, at the moment, of Nauru and Tonga. This option might appeal to microstates if substantial institutional and programmatic benefits were available to them without membership, or, conversely, if the costs of participation were too great. A major stumbling block for this approach is that the very organizations that most need to restrict their membership, such as the United Nations, possess the greatest attraction to the smaller states. Abstentionism, therefore, may be rendered more practicable if it is induced by various forms of dissuasion, for example, prescribing probationary waiting periods, requiring compliance with specified standards and admission requisites, excluding microstates from certain participatory functions, or increasing the amount of their financial contributions to onerous levels. These could be used in conjunction with an offer of institutional benefits for not joining.

An exclusionist approach would have the international organizations expressly prohibiting or otherwise restraining the affiliation of microstates by fixing precise admission criteria that transcend mere independence, commitment to constitutive acts, and formal initiation of the admission process.[27] This requires firm standards for participation, perhaps based on a combination of such factors as population size and density, economic resources and levels of production and foreign trade, standard of living, financial and political stability, ability to further the welfare of the organization and its members, and the like. However, it would be difficult to produce an acceptable admission formula, even for the most objective or readily quantifiable factors, to say nothing of those that rely upon subjective assessment. Whatever the prescription, many would argue that it is too late, that it would discriminate against future members, or that it would transgress presumed intangible rights.

Alternatives unlikely to be accepted, though worthy of consideration, are such variants as fixing the maximum membership size of the international organization by predetermining to admit only specified new states as they become independent,[28] or, in the case of the United

[27] One of the looser arrangements was provided in Article 4 of the Charter of the Organization of American States, which simply specified that "all American states that ratify the present Charter are members of the Organization," not even requiring its confirmatory action. Subsequently this was rectified, establishing procedures for application and admission action by the council of the organization.

[28] The practice of predetermining participants is not entirely foreign to treaty making and the establishment of international organizations. While it is conceivable that treaties may specify states not parties to their negotiation as potential signatories and ratifiers, such stipulation is more common for the constitutive acts of international organizations. For example, the League of Nations Covenant empowered states named in its annex that had not participated in its devisement to become original league members upon their accession to the covenant. See League of Nations Covenant, Article 1, paragraph 1.

Although Poland did not attend the San Francisco Conference in 1945, it was given the opportunity to sign the Charter and become an original member of the United Nations. The formula employed specified that not only nations participating in the conference but also others that had previously signed the United Nations Declaration of 1942 could become original members. This stipulation did not designate the states by name. See U.S. Department of State,

Nations, for the permanent members of the Security Council to employ their veto power against membership applications to enhance the future welfare of the organization rather than for political reasons. Admission, rightly or wrongly, is essentially a political act on the part of the international organization, and the history of such agencies as the United Nations is rich in accounts of individual member states supporting or rejecting applications on the basis of political bias. Despite the fact that in 1948 the International Court of Justice handed down an advisory opinion that the conditions set forth in the Charter constitute an exhaustive and sufficient enumeration of qualifications for membership, there is, as noted earlier, the proviso that, in the judgment of the organization—which, ultimately, means its members—the applicant must be *able* and *willing* to carry out the obligations of membership. Therefore, should a permanent member of the Security Council judge that an applicant is unsuitable on those grounds, it could theoretically cast its veto without the onus of political bias.[29]

From the political perspective of the United States, rather than veto the admission of microstate applicants, it might be deemed preferable deliberately to change the qualitative character of U.N. membership by promoting the admission of large numbers of new—and friendly—Caribbean and Oceanic states. The addition of forty to fifty such countries to membership, although aggravating the microstate problem, might enhance the voting power of the democracies on East-West and other ideological questions. However, it also might have the effect of strengthening the current majority of the Third World, the developing nations, and the more economically deprived countries on an array of anticolonial, economic reform, and similar issues.

The choice between restraining proliferation and serving a favorable voting majority is a vexing one for the United States and other industrialized powers. It must be remembered, in the United Nations the veto is exercisable by East and West alike. On balance, it may be more prudent simply to continue supporting the admission of promising candidates than it would be to accept the responsibility, and face the criticism, for vetoing admissions on the basis of unilateral adjudgment of membership qualification.

Charter of the United Nations: Report to the President on the Results of the San Francisco Conference . . . June 26, 1945 (Washington, D.C.: Government Printing Office, Department of State Publication 2349, 1945), pp. 46-47.

[29] In most organizations constitutional authorization and institutional processes for vetoing membership are lacking, so restrictive policy and action have to be negotiated. In a few agencies such as the North Atlantic Treaty Organization, the veto exists automatically by virtue of the rule of unanimity.

Even though it may be concluded that few of these suggestions for restricting membership expansion appear to be realistic for existing international organizations, some could be applied in devising future agencies. A few of these options—such as a probationary period, procedural admission restraints, higher financial assessments, or a fixed membership size—might be instituted administratively or informally. However, some aspects of these proposals, certainly any major redefinition of membership criteria and participation rights, require constitutional amendment. Efforts to introduce changes of this nature would be viewed as anti-universalist and discriminatory, and therefore politically sensitive. At best, if enough of the larger powers stood together, theoretically they could enact essential constitutional reforms, and the smaller states that refused to accept them could withdraw from the organization.

Institutional Reorganization and Realignment. An essentially different approach is to reorganize individual international organizations or to restructure the entire system. Judicious realignment might ameliorate a good many mechanical, structural, and procedural difficulties. The shifting of functions and policy-making power from large plenary forums to small, nucleus councils and committees could reduce the quantity and complexity of voting, realign decision-making authority, and convey a greater voice to those countries that bear the larger responsibility.[30]

Internal realignment is especially pertinent to such organizations as the United Nations and the Organization of American States. It might be achieved in the former if the General Assembly met less frequently (every three or five years) and a substantial share of its functions were transferred to the Security Council; or, leaving the latter unchanged, if an intermediate organ were created to meet more frequently than the assembly, with a substantial share of assembly functions transferred to it and the major powers guaranteed representation. In the Organization of American States, under a sweeping application of the principle of equality, all members are represented in all of its major organs—the General Assembly, the ministerial-level Organ of Consultation, the three principal councils, and the Juridical Committee. If membership increases, each new micro-member will be

---

[30] This institutional process is common to many international organizations, in which equal and full representation and voting authority accrue to all members in plenary organs that meet only occasionally, while the main business of the organization is handled on a more frequent if not permanent basis by small, nucleus agencies. In some organizations the latter function at the ministerial level, in which case decisions usually require unanimity.

able to take its place beside the major Western Hemisphere powers in each of these forums, which are all apt to have as many legally equal participants as there are members in the organization. Restructuring at least the Organ of Consultation and the Permanent Council would help to redefine the locus of authority and responsibility and might produce less diluted and more positive results. Structural modification could help to bridge some of the problems resulting from extensive microstate proliferation, but much of it would require constitutional revision, which can be achieved only if all of the major powers and a sufficient number of other states unite in support of the change.

Internal reorganization is not a likely, nor in some cases a necessary, solution for those international agencies that are already structured to concentrate substantial authority in nucleus councils, or for the financial institutions in which representation, authority, and voting are constitutionally aligned.[31]

A more sweeping approach involves reorganizing much if not all of the present system, perhaps by downgrading the United Nations and some regional agencies, and paralleling or overlaying them with new international machinery planned, established, and controlled by a limited group of states to exercise some of the more important political functions of the international community. New institutions could be restricted solely to specified states, or could consist of a combination of both individual and representative states, the latter coalescing regional or bloc interests. Or, serving much the same purpose, the United States and other major powers could withdraw from existing organizations like the United Nations, or reduce their level of participation, and form their own more restricted institutions. Assuming that this step were taken by the principal financial contributors to the United Nations and other major agencies, the viability and influence of the organizations would be curtailed. Because such revolutionary action would remold the fundamental international institutional system, which has taken decades to fabricate, it appears to be an unlikely prospect.

Weighted Representation and Voting. An option that is frequently suggested to rectify the relationship of authority and responsibility rather than to forestall membership growth is to institute weighted representation and voting. The principle of proportional representation and voting power is fundamental to contemporary European

---

[31] Nor is it necessary for the International Court of Justice, in which the problem of membership proliferation is not critical.

organizations. Not only is it characteristic of the parliamentary forums of the Council of Europe, the European communities, and the Western European Union,[32] but it is also incorporated by the Economic and Social Committee and in the voting arrangement of the Council of Ministers of the European Economic Community.[33] Weighted representation is similarly embodied in the decision-making mechanisms of the International Bank, the International Monetary Fund, and other global and regional financial and development institutions, in which, as noted earlier, national governments exercise voting authority commensurate with the funds they commit. In these cases voting arrangements were carefully determined in advance when their acceptability was related directly to the overriding issue of the very existence of the organization and individual state affiliation.

If weighted voting were introduced into the United Nations and other organizations, it could be based on population, on financial contribution, or on some combination of these and other factors. A formula based solely on financial contributions would give the United States compelling voting power and would reduce that of more than half of the member states to infinitesimal amounts. A formula based on population would of course give the most strength to the People's Republic of China, would place the United States among the four countries with the highest voting power, and again would miniaturize that of the smaller states. In order to accommodate the low-vote states, the United States and other large contributors or populous states would acquire very high numbers or percentages of votes, or, inversely, the small states would be reduced to minute fractional votes.

Neither of these alternatives appears to be likely or desirable. It may be more equitable and would be more acceptable to categorize voting authority, with the smallest states possessing a single vote, others wielding two, three, and more votes, and the highest voting powers equated as a category. This would provide leveling at both the base and apex of the scale.[34] Or some form of grouping of states for voting purposes could be instituted, requiring either advance caucusing and the determination of single joint votes or the splitting of votes. Or the formula could provide an individual vote to each of the principal powers and combine other states into groups, to each of

[32] Votes in the Consultative Assembly of the Council of Europe range from 3 to 18 per member and total 147. Representation in the European Parliament runs from 6 to 36, totaling nearly 200 votes.

[33] Votes of council members are weighted from two to ten.

[34] This system is used in some national parliamentary chambers, such as the West German *Bundesrat*, in which each *Land* (state) possesses from three to five votes.

which a vote would be allocated. The acceptability and effectiveness of decision making by such voting processes depends on the roles ascribed to the individual members and groups of states.

Weighted voting could rectify serious imbalances in the relation of responsibility, votes, and contributions. The main drawbacks to it are that it contravenes the ingrained principle of legal equality in international political institutions, that it necessitates constitutional revision, that states naturally resist diminution of their voting power, and that, unless a realistic and workable formula for applying it can be devised and agreed upon by the major powers, it cannot even approach negotiability. Legal equality is virtually sacrosanct with smaller powers, and representation and voting power are among the most difficult issues to resolve in organizing political forums. It follows that weighted voting is unrealistic at present for the United Nations, the Organization of American States, and similar international agencies. However, because it is operative in some global and regional institutions, it cannot be completely discounted either in principle or in fabricating new international organizations, and in the long run it might warrant serious consideration in the United Nations as well.

Special Forms of Membership. The most widely suggested proposal to resolve the membership issue is to provide special forms of limited participation and status in international organizations specifically for microstates and other small countries. Suggestions range from ordinary and strengthened observerships to joint representation and associate membership. Some forms of restricted participation are already common and, if instituted by the United Nations and other agencies, could help to mitigate the micro-member problem.

The most obvious alternative, the observership, is already available in many international organizations, including the United Nations, and requires little modification of present practice. Although, in general, there are great differences in its nature, methods of functioning, and purposes among international organizations, an observership affords opportunities for contact and consultation, access to officials and documents, presence at sessions, and indirect influence, even though the observer state may not be empowered to participate freely in debate or to vote. Nonmember delegations are expected to bear their own expenses, and their participation may be permanent or ad hoc, direct or indirect, formal or informal, extensive or limited.[35]

[35] The accrediting of observership missions to international organizations (and to international conferences) by national governments, political factions, and

Some organizations have recognized substantial numbers of observership missions, and the United Nations should be able to define a strengthened quasi-member status that is sufficiently dignified and rewarding to be attractive to microstates and other small countries as a substitute for full affiliation. A comprehensive program for observer missions could be provided by separate U.N. agencies tailored specifically to look after their interests and needs, and such special treatment might offset the loss of prestige suffered by forgoing full membership.

Another possibility, suggested occasionally but largely untried, consists of grouping small states for representational purposes, either on a voluntary or on an enforced basis. This could restrict potential growth in the number of participants and votes, but it would raise thorny questions for the states concerned. For example, who should represent the group, and how would he be selected, and for how long? How would the policy positions of collaborating states be coordinated, who would instruct the representative, and how would his vote be determined? How would the financial obligation of the combined members be distributed among the participating states? Only those small states that freely agree on common objectives, interests, and policies are apt to be able to compromise their differences sufficiently to accept and benefit from such amalgamated membership. But what happens when the parties to joint arrangements disagree enough to discourage cooperation? Small state grouping is really a disguised—and far less workable—form of imposing fractional votes on low contributors, and its chances for successful and helpful operation seem negligible.

A final possibility, most frequently proposed as a solution to the problem of microstate affiliation with the United Nations, is to create a new intermediate status. Some international agencies have long recognized the desirability of embracing entities other than fully established states and have provided an associate membership status to accommodate them. For example, the International Telecommunication and Universal Postal Unions permitted metropolitan governments to affiliate their colonies and dependent possessions on such terms. In the postal organization associate members exercised voting rights, were required to contribute to its financial support, and were com-

public and private international agencies is well established in diplomatic practice, but differs widely from one organization to another. For a comprehensive analysis of the observership role, see Jung Gun Kim, "Non-Member Participation in International Organizations" (Ph.D. dissertation, University of Maryland, 1965).

parable to other members except for the designation and manner of their affiliation, but this membership arrangement was changed considerably after World War II. The Telecommunication Union enables dependent territories not fully responsible for the conduct of their foreign relations to become associate members, and they may participate in its plenary and administrative conferences and are required to contribute financially, but are not empowered to vote. Several other specialized agencies of the United Nations also permit such affiliation, but usually this is a temporary status and is eventually converted into full membership.[36] Similarly special arrangements are negotiated by the European Economic Community with the former dependencies of its members, affording them associate status in the Common Market, and separate machinery was developed to manage their interrelations. The European community also provides associate status for countries like Greece, which, unready for full membership, prefer a slower process of affiliation.

With few exceptions, the limits on associate status usually include the denial of decision-making authority, and may also apply to balloting for officers of the organization, office holding, and the benefit of certain services, and it may entail restrictions on the right to be heard, either on prescribed matters or in certain organs of the organization. Limited status could be made available to small states on a voluntary basis, or tendered as the only form of membership (other than observership) open to them, or promoted indirectly by raising the level of the minimum financial contributions of regular members.

Generally conceded as advantages of associate membership are selective participation, the application of programmatic benefits, and at least some voice and influence, without major financial responsibility. The international organization gains by stabilizing membership and forestalling the extension of microstate votes and the dilution of authority of those who bear the greatest responsibility. A major difficulty may arise from the sensitivities of states to what they might regard as second-class membership. While associate status may have been acceptable to dependent territories and emerging states, or may be applicable in the European communities, it is less attractive to new microstates in a system that has for years been functioning as a forum of legal equals. Nevertheless, they would have little discretion in the matter if the existing members of these organizations provided no alternative.

---

[36] For example, the Food and Agriculture Organization, the Intergovernmental Maritime Consultative Organization, the World Meteorological Organization, and UNESCO.

The major difficulty with this option is its feasibility. Some analysts argue that institution of a new class of membership, unless constitutionally authorized, is illegal and requires formal amendatory action. In organizations possessing simple amending procedures this is relatively easy, but in others, such as the United Nations—in which Security Council permanent members possess a ratification veto—and those which require unanimous amendatory approval, it is far more difficult. Nevertheless, if the will exists to establish an associate membership status, either it will be possible to employ the amending process or a way will be found to reinterpret the constitutive act to authorize the change. Even though the issue may be held to be legal, in actuality its resolution would be determined by political considerations.

Policy Determination

Analysis of microstate participation can be viewed from the perspectives of the community of nations, the international organizations, the smaller states, and other powers including the United States. Perceptions of the issues and the solutions will vary kaleidoscopically with the perspective. National policy makers and international institutions must harmonize and compromise a heterogeneous—and often competitive if not antithetical—assortment of national and international desires, interests, and benefits.

The corporate community of nations is faced with the whole complex of problems resulting from three decades of small-state proliferation. Affected are diplomatic relations and conferences, treaty making, and membership in, and functioning of, international organizations. Permeating the considerations of the world community are the essence and practical effects of decolonization, self-determination, self-governance, independence, sovereignty, legal equality, and universality. Inaction by the community would insure continued expansion of statehood, aggravating the difficulties. Attempts to limit the independence race, to alter the existing composition of the world community or the nature of statehood, or to modify the doctrines of legal equality and universality would be considered revolutionary in concept, even if evolutionary in effect. The most positive options are alternative agencies, forums, and procedures to facilitate future development, establish some minimum standard for statehood and participation in global affairs, and overlay existing instrumentalities with superior agencies and processes that accord more fully with political realities.

The perspective of international organizations, though similar to that of the global community in some respects, is more restricted. Multinational political agencies can restrict microstate affiliation, but in and of themselves they do not control statehood, notwithstanding that the United Nations, among others, has piloted the rush to independence and international status. International agencies are daily confronted with pragmatic problems of operations and administration, decision making, financial resources, equity of interrelating authority, responsibility, and contribution among members, and capacity to fulfill objectives, all of which are affected by proliferation.

However, international organizations have several options for effectively stabilizing growth and improving their functioning. Some may be simpler to institute than others, such as dissuading or excluding small states from membership, and offering or imposing on them special forms of affiliation. Structural and functional reorganization could restrict the role of the smaller powers, but would be difficult to put into effect. Restructuring could modify the dogma of legal equality and align contribution to responsibility. To imbue such change in philosophy with some degree of permanence, organizations could employ a variety of processes, including weighted representation and voting. None of these options is inherently foreign to international organizations, to be automatically discounted as exceeding the realm of possibility.

The nature of the problem from the viewpoint of the microstates is of course quite different. Their objectives, beyond gaining independence and membership in the family of nations, are to maintain their status and retain the benefits they derive from existing institutions and practices. Their policy, therefore, focuses on preserving an environment that confirms their independence and the principles of legal equality and universality, accords them prestige, affords them participatory flexibility, provides them maximum benefits at minimum cost, and guarantees them adequate voice and voting authority in world affairs. Many of the options that would most advance the welfare of the community of nations would contravene the interests of the micro-members. The latter, consequently, will defend the status quo. The more microstates that emerge, the stronger they will be in collectively maintaining current institutions and procedures, preserving their advantages, and perpetuating the inequalities of representation and responsibility.

The United States and other larger powers are confronted with a community of states growing rapidly through the admission of ostensible equals who in practical fact are nothing of the sort. This poses a complex of problems related to expanding diplomatic communities with more taxing needs and demands, more conflicting policy, more extensive and complicated mechanisms, more splintering of interests, and more mercurial centers of economic and political power. The most serious blunder would be to ignore the problem or to decide cavalierly that nothing can or should be done about it.

The United States and other powers must determine how far they are willing to bear the burdens of unilateral diplomatic representation, adopt and underwrite new techniques to furnish representational service to the smaller states, exempt them from treaty making and overt commitment to the rule of law, permit them to participate as equals in international conferences, and enable them to affiliate with and possibly control if not dominate major international organizations.

Some contend that the "democratization" of the family of nations should continue unrestrained, that the better endowed states are under obligation, moral if not political, to support the less fortunate, and that, after all, equals are equals. Others, less naive, respond that some "equals" are simply more equal than others, that the current situation is getting out of hand, and that failure to seek reform could be disastrous. Though appreciating its difficulty, they do not shrink from the task of weighing complicated and sometimes risky alternatives to preserve the orderly conduct of world affairs.[37]

In the course of time, initiating reform may be increasingly difficult, yet more crucial. Some of the options now available may well be foreclosed by the flow of events if not consciously kept open. Procrastination or inaction cannot avoid risks or avert the necessity of concrete decisions. "In the real world," Walter Lippmann once said, "there are always equations which have to be adjusted between the possible and the desired. . . . Valid choices are limited to the question where, not whether, the opposing terms of the equation are to be brought into equilibrium."[38] Like it or not, microstate proliferation is eroding the equilibrium in the community of nations, corrective actions are available, and sooner or later the hard decisions will have to be made.

---

[37] While not delving into matters of membership proliferation and the relation of voting power to financial contribution, the Senate has undertaken to examine and reassess the role of the United States in international organizations. It is particularly concerned with their missions, effectiveness, and excesses, the legitimization of block positions and deliberate politicization of issues, the benefits achievable by the United States from its financial contributions, the systemization of priorities, and the desirability of American policy review. See U.S. Senate, *U.S. Participation in International Organizations*, 95th Congress, 1st sesson, 1977.

[38] *The Public Philosophy* (New York: Mentor, 1955), p. 40.

APPENDIX TABLES

Appendix A

COMMUNITY OF NATIONS

Country	Location[a]	Indepen-dence[b]	Square Miles[c] (thou-sands)	Popula-tion[d] (thou-sands)	Micro	Small	Medium	Large
Afghanistan	Asia	*	251.0	17,480			E	
Albania	Europe	*	11.1	1,626		D		
Algeria	M.E.	1962	920.0	11,822			E	
Angola	Africa	1975	481.6	5,673			E	
Argentina	W.H.	*	1,072.1	23,362			E	
Australia	Oceania	*	2,968.0	12,756			E	
Austria	Europe	*	32.4	7,456			E	
Bahamas	W.H.	1973	4.4	175	B			
Bahrain	M.E.	1971	(231)	216	B			
Bangladesh	Asia	1972	55.1	71,317				G
Barbados	W.H.	1966	(166)	238	B			
Belgium	Europe	*	11.8	9,651			E	
Benin (Dahomey)	Africa	1960	43.5	2,106		D		
Bhutan	Asia	Semi-independent	19.3	1,035		D		
Bolivia	W.H.	*	424.2	2,704		D		
Botswana (Bechuanaland)	Africa	1966	222.0	609		C		
Brazil	W.H.	*	3,286.5	92,342				H
Bulgaria	Europe	*	42.8	8,228			E	
Burma	Asia	1948	261.8	28,886			F	
Burundi	Africa	1962	10.7	3,350		D		
Byelorussian S.S.R.	Europe	—	80.2	9,002			E	
Cameroon	Africa	1960	183.6	5,017			E	
Canada	W.H.	*	3,851.8	21,568			E	
Cape Verde Islands	Africa	1975	1.6	272	B			
Central African Republic	Africa	1960	241.3	1,612		D		
Chad	Africa	1960	495.8	3,254		D		
Chile	W.H.	*	286.4	8,835			E	
China, People's Republic	Asia	1949	3,691.5	772,676				J
China, Republic of	Asia	*	13.6	14,500			E	
Colombia	W.H.	*	455.4	17,485			E	
Comoro Islands	Africa	1975	(902)	244	B			
Congo (Brazzaville)	Africa	1960	132.0	1,300		D		
Costa Rica	W.H.	*	19.7	1,846		D		
Cuba	W.H.	*	44.2	8,553			E	
Cyprus	Europe	1960	3.6	578		C		
Czechoslovakia	Europe	*	49.4	14,345			E	

Diplomatic Missions [f]	U.S. Mission to [g]	Mission to U.S. [h]	International Organization Membership [i]		Bilateral Treaties with U.S.	50 Selected Multilateral Treaties [j]	45 Selected International Conferences [k]
			U.N. system	Other			
46 (19)	X	X	15	0	3	20	18
54			9	1	6	13	19
46 (41)	X	X	16	2	1	24	10
—			1	0	0	0	0
81 (68)	X	X	17	3	34	33	41
68	X	X	17	3	45	43	44
140 (57)	X	X	16	3	37	43	27
—*	X	X	8	0	25	20	2
—*	X		9	0	2	8	4
71	X	X	14	1	6	5	5
—*	X	X	13	1	18	28	3
132	X	X	17	3	46	43	45
—*	X	X	14	1	4	22	6
2			4	0	0	2	3
19	X	X	14	2	31	19	30
—*	X	X	9	1	5	23	4
73	X	X	17	3	58	39	44
100 (59)	X	X	13	2	8	39	25
27	X	X	16	1	13	18	19
—*	X	X	13	2	6	20	8
—			10	1	0	26	26
—*	X	X	17	2	3	25	8
127	X	X	17	3	186	43	44
—			2	0	0	0	0
—*	X	X	13	1	3	24	8
—*	X	X	14	1	2	12	8
59	X	X	17	3	41	30	40
97	X[l]	X[l]	5	0	0	5	3
32	X	X	11	2	61	36	35
39 (38)	X	X	16	2	43	27	38
—			3	0	0	0	0
—*			14	1	5	14	11
19	X	X	15	1	19	26	32
51			13	3	30	32	37
11	X	X	17	1	14	37	6
88 (70)	X	X	13	3	17	40	39

Country	Location [a]	Indepen-dence [b]	Square Miles [c] (thousands)	Population [d] (thousands)	Micro	Small	Medium	Large
					Category [e]			
Denmark	Europe	*	16.6	4,938		D		
Dominican Republic	W.H.	*	18.7	4,006		D		
Ecuador	W.H.	*	105.7	6,501			E	
Egypt	M.E.	*	386.9	30,076			F	
El Salvador	W.H.	*	8.3	3,549		D		
Equatorial Guinea	Africa	1968	10.8	246	B			
Ethiopia	Africa	*	457.1	25,248			F	
Fiji	Oceania	1970	7.1	477		C		
Finland	Europe	*	130.1	4,622		D		
France	Europe	*	213.0	49,779			F	
Gabon	Africa	1960	102.3	449		C		
Gambia, The	Africa	1965	4.0	493		C		
Germany, Democratic Rep.	Europe	1949	40.6	17,068			E	
Germany, Federal Rep.	Europe	*	95.8	60,651				G
Ghana	Africa	1957	92.1	8,559			E	
Greece	Europe	*	50.5	8,769			E	
Grenada	W.H.	1974	(133)	95	A			
Guatemala	W.H.	*	42.0	5,175			E	
Guinea	Africa	1958	94.9	2,570		D		
Guinea-Bissau	Africa	1974	13.9	487		C		
Guyana	W.H.	1966	83.0	714		C		
Haiti	W.H.	*	10.7	4,244		D		
Honduras	W.H.	*	43.3	2,654		D		
Hungary	Europe	*	35.9	10,322			E	
Iceland	Europe	1944	39.7	205	B			
India	Asia	1947	1,262.0	547,950				J
Indonesia	Asia	1949	735.3	118,460				I
Iran	M.E.	*	636.4	25,785			F	
Iraq	M.E.	*	167.6	8,047			E	
Ireland	Europe	*	26.6	2,978		D		
Israel	M.E.	1948	8.0	3,124		D		
Italy	Europe	*	116.3	54,025				G
Ivory Coast	Africa	1960	124.5	3,100		D		
Jamaica	W.H.	1962	4.4	1,865		D		
Japan	Asia	*	143.6	104,665				I
Jordan	M.E.	1946	37.3	1,706		D		
Kenya	Africa	1963	225.0	10,943			E	
Khmer Rep. (Cambodia)	Asia	1949	70.0	5,729			E	

Diplomatic Missions [f]	U.S. Mission to [g]	Mission to U.S. [h]	International Organization Membership [i]		Bilateral Treaties with U.S.	50 Selected Multilateral Treaties [j]	45 Selected International Conferences [k]
			U.N. system	Other			
106 (105)	X	X	17	3	46	48	41
33	X	X	16	3	26	30	36
29	X	X	16	2	31	35	36
79	X	X	17	3	29	39	43
37 (25)	X	X	15	2	22	24	31
—*	X		9	1	0	7	2
27	X	X	15	0	27	24	25
—*	X	X	11	1	15	34	4
92 (43)	X	X	17	3	23	46	33
111	X	X	17	3	69	42	45
—*	X	X	16	1	2	21	7
6	X		10	1	12	24	4
76	X	X	11	0	1	27	4
112	X	X	17	3	79	44	24
37	X	X	16	1	18	35	14
67 (47)	X	X	17	3	64	41	43
—*	X	m	3	0	12	13	1
30 (28)	X	X	15	1	27	28	32
—*	X	X	13	0	12	11	10
—*		m	5	0	0	4	1
10	X	X	14	1	18	24	4
24	X	X	15	3	18	27	25
21	X	X	15	1	28	21	24
100 (63)	X	X	13	3	27	40	25
41 (9)	X	X	16	3	32	34	22
124	X	X	17	3	45	36	42
50	X	X	17	2	31	22	29
44 (36)	X	X	16	2	31	34	37
47 (30)			16	2	14	32	30
23	X	X	17	2	19	37	33
65	X	X	17	3	39	33	26
134 (103)	X	X	17	3	68	40	35
12	X	X	17	2	5	28	10
37	X	X	14	1	21	34	7
96	X	X	17	3	85	36	30
29	X	X	17	1	12	28	15
51	X	X	17	1	8	29	9
17			15	1	8	24	15

Country	Location[a]	Indepen-dence[b]	Square Miles[c] (thou-sands)	Popula-tion[d] (thou-sands)	Category[e]			
					Micro	Small	Medium	Large
Korea, Democratic People's Republic	Asia	1945	46.8	14,281			E	
Korea, Republic of	Asia	1948	38.0	31,466			F	
Kuwait	M.E.	1961	7.8	738		C		
Laos	Asia	1949	91.4	3,106		D		
Lebanon	M.E.	1943	4.0	2,126		D		
Lesotho (Basutoland)	Africa	1966	11.7	852		C		
Liberia	Africa	*	43.0	1,016		D		
Libya	M.E.	1951	679.5	2,257		D		
Luxembourg	Europe	*	(999)	340		C		
Madagascar (Malagasy)	Africa	1960	230.0	6,200			E	
Malawi	Africa	1964	45.7	4,040		D		
Malaysia	Asia	1957	128.3	10,442			E	
Maldives	Asia	1965	(115)	122	B			
Mali	Africa	1960	464.9	3,485		D		
Malta	Europe	1964	(122)	316		C		
Mauritania	Africa	1960	419.2	1,030		D		
Mauritius	Africa	1968	(787)	851		C		
Mexico	W.H.	*	761.6	48,225			F	
Mongolia	Asia	*	604.2	1,198		D		
Morocco	M.E.	1956	172.0	15,379			E	
Mozambique	Africa	1975	303.1	8,234			E	
Nauru	Oceania	1968	(8)	6	A			
Nepal	Asia	1947	54.4	11,556			E	
Netherlands	Europe	*	14.0	13,046			E	
New Zealand	Oceania	*	103.7	2,863		D		
Nicaragua	W.H.	*	57.1	1,878		D		
Niger	Africa	1960	489.2	2,502		D		
Nigeria	Africa	1960	356.7	55,670				G
Norway	Europe	*	125.2	3,888		D		
Oman	M.E.	1970	81.0	678		C		
Pakistan	Asia	1947	342.8	64,892				G
Panama	W.H.	*	28.8	1,428		D		
Papua New Guinea	Oceania	1975	183.5	2,481		D		
Paraguay	W.H.	*	157.0	2,354		D		
Peru	W.H.	*	496.2	13,572			E	
Philippines	Asia	1946	115.7	36,684			F	
Poland	Europe	*	120.4	32,642			F	

Diplomatic Missions[f]		U.S. Mission to[g]	Mission to U.S.[h]	International Organization Membership[i]		Bilateral Treaties with U.S.	50 Selected Multilateral Treaties[j]	45 Selected International Conferences[k]
				U.N. system	Other			
64				3	0	0	5	2
81	(51)	X	X	13	2	55	27	19
43		X	X	16	1	4	23	10
38	(12)	X	X	13	1	4	26	11
43		X	X	16	2	16	37	32
—*		X	X	12	1	6	22	5
39		X	X	16	0	30	26	31
33		X	X	16	1	3	18	13
16	(10)	X	X	16	3	22	35	33
30		X	X	17	1	8	35	9
26		X	X	15	1	7	24	2
33		X	X	16	2	18	29	12
—*		X		8	1	0	8	0
—*		X	X	14	1	7	27	9
49		X	X	12	3	13	30	3
—*		X	X	16	1	3	13	8
—*		X	X	15	2	10	33	6
75	(70)	X	X	17	2	64	41	41
58				10	0	0	21	10
35		X	X	17	1	16	36	19
—				3	0	0	0	0
—		X		2	0	2	12	1
56	(13)	X	X	14	0	7	23	10
136	(82)	X	X	17	3	57	44	44
43		X	X	15	2	24	43	37
25		X	X	14	3	31	25	29
—*		X	X	15	1	4	26	8
46		X	X	16	1	11	38	9
101	(44)	X	X	17	3	41	47	44
—*		X	X	14	0	2	9	4
95		X	X	16	3	40	34	30
53	(36)	X	X	16	2	45	28	35
—*			X	3	0	0	1	0
25	(22)	X	X	15	1	36	29	21
61		X	X	16	3	38	23	37
42		X	X	16	1	89	35	35
92		X	X	13	3	42	39	41

Appendix A (continued)

Country	Location[a]	Independence[b]	Square Miles (thousands)	Population[d] (thousands)	Category[e] Micro	Small	Medium	Large
Portugal	Europe	*	35.3	8,668			E	
Qatar	M.E.	1971	4.0	100	B			
Romania	Europe	*	91.7	19,103			E	
Rwanda	Africa	1962	10.2	3,736		D		
São Tomé and Príncipe	Africa	1975	(372)	74	A			
Saudi Arabia	M.E.	*	873.0	7,965			E	
Senegal	Africa	1960	76.1	3,110		D		
Sierra Leone	Africa	1961	28.0	2,180		D		
Singapore	Asia	1965	(225)	2,075		D		
Somalia	Africa	1960	246.2	2,941		D		
South Africa	Africa	*	471.8	21,448			E	
Spain	Europe	*	194.9	30,041			F	
Sri Lanka (Ceylon)	Asia	1948	25.3	12,711			E	
Sudan	M.E.	1956	967.5	14,172			E	
Surinam (Dutch Guiana)	W.H.	1975	63.3	385		C		
Swaziland	Africa	1968	6.7	375		C		
Sweden	Europe	*	173.7	8,077			E	
Switzerland	Europe	*	15.9	6,270			E	
Syria	M.E.	1944	71.5	6,305			E	
Tanzania	Africa	1961	362.8	12,313			E	
Thailand (Siam)	Asia	*	198.5	34,397			F	
Togo	Africa	1960	21.9	1,954		D		
Tonga (Friendly Islands)	Oceania	1970	(270)	77	A			
Trinidad and Tobago	W.H.	1962	2.0	945		C		
Tunisia	M.E.	1956	63.4	4,533		D		
Turkey	M.E.	*	301.4	35,667			F	
Uganda	Africa	1962	91.1	9,549			E	
Ukranian S.S.R.	Europe	—	232.0	47,127			F	
U.S.S.R.	Europe	*	8,647.3	241,720				J
United Arab Emirates	M.E.	1971	32.0	179	B			
United Kingdom	Europe	*	94.2	55,506				G
United States	W.H.	*	3,628.2	203,235				J
Upper Volta	Africa	1960	105.9	4,300		D		
Uruguay	W.H.	*	68.5	2,596		D		
Vatican City (Holy See)	Europe	*	(0.17)	0.9	A			
Venezuela	W.H.	*	352.1	10,722			E	
Vietnam, Democratic Rep.	Asia	1954	60.2	15,917			E	
Vietnam, Republic of[n]	Asia	1949/1954	66.3	18,809			E	

Diplomatic Missions [f]	U.S. Mission to [g]	Mission to U.S. [h]	International Organization Membership [i]		Bilateral Treaties with U.S.	50 Selected Multilateral Treaties [j]	45 Selected International Conferences [k]
			U.N. system	Other			
47	X	X	15	3	29	36	33
—*	X	X	11	1	0	7	4
104	X	X	15	3	20	40	26
—*	X	X	13	2	6	25	8
—			2	0	0	0	0
28	X	X	15	1	13	19	20
—*	X	X	17	2	5	27	10
16	X	X	16	1	16	26	7
32	X	X	14	2	14	25	3
15	X	X	14	0	3	18	4
25 (22)	X	X	13	2	20	35	34
98 (75)	X	X	17	3	52	40	27
56	X	X	16	2	22	30	24
58 (26)	X	X	17	2	8	19	11
—			3	0	0	0	2
—*	X	X	11	2	11	24	5
127 (72)	X	X	17	3	28	43	37
120	X	X	12	3	21	41	34
53	X	X	17	1	10	27	24
63	X	X	15	1	7	26	7
40 (38)	X	X	17	2	24	26	29
—*	X	X	15	1	5	20	6
—*	X		2	1	6	23	1
13	X	X	15	1	24	34	8
36	X	X	17	1	20	38	19
61	X	X	17	3	43	33	41
12		X	16	2	4	24	10
—			10	1	0	26	26
116	X	X	12	2	46	44	36
—*	X	X	12	0	0	9	5
134	X	X	17	3	128	47	45
131 (122)			17	3	—	45	45
—*	X	X	14	2	3	18	7
43	X	X	15	3	20	28	36
77			3	0	1	18	23
49	X	X	14	2	24	30	39
25			0	0	1	3	1
33			14	1	33	25	19

Appendix A (continued)

Country	Location[a]	Independence[b]	Square Miles[c] (thousands)	Population[d] (thousands)	Category[e] Micro	Small	Medium	Large
Western Samoa	Oceania	1962	1.1	147	B			
Yemen Arab Rep. (San'a)	M.E.	*	75.3	6,062			E	
Yemen People's Rep. (Aden)	M.E.	1967	111.0	1,590		D		
Yugoslavia	Europe	*	98.8	20,523			E	
Zaire (Congo/Leopoldville)	Africa	1960	905.1	12,769			E	
Zambia	Africa	1964	290.7	4,057		D		
Total 155	—	—	—	—	16	63	63	13

[a] Geographic areas include: Western Hemisphere (W.H.), Europe, Mideast and North Africa (M.E.), sub-Saharan Africa (Africa), Asia and Indian Ocean (Asia), and Oceania. Location of countries is based on U.N. and Department of State allocations.

[b] Dates indicate year of independence; asterisk (*) denotes pre-World War II status (as of 1940). For dates of U.S. commencement of diplomatic relations, see Elmer Plischke, *United States Diplomats and Their Missions: A Profile of American Diplomatic Emissaries since 1778* (Washington, D.C.: American Enterprise Institute, 1975), Appendices A-1, A-2, A-5, and A-14.

[c] Figures are rounded to nearest 100 square miles. Figures in parentheses give specific area for countries having areas of less than 1,000 square miles.

[d] Figures are rounded to nearest 1,000.

[e] For population categories, see p. 18.

[f] Figures indicate number of diplomatic missions to other governments headed by ambassadors and ministers. Where discrepancy exists, the number of chiefs of mission is given in parentheses; the difference represents multiple diplomatic accreditation, with individual emissaries commissioned simultaneously to more than one foreign country. Figures combine embassies and legations, but do not include consulates. A dash (—) denotes no missions or information unavailable, and a dash with an asterisk (—*) denotes missions to the United Kingdom, the United States, or both.

[g] X indicates that the United States accredits a diplomatic mission to the country.

[h] X indicates that the country listed maintains a diplomatic mission accredited to the United States.

[i] The names and membership totals of these organizations are given in Chapter 6.

[j] For a list of the fifty selected multilateral treaties, see Table 9.

Diplomatic Missions [f]	U.S. Mission to [g]	Mission to U.S. [h]	International Organization Membership [i]		Bilateral Treaties with U.S.	50 Selected Multilateral Treaties [j]	45 Selected International Conferences [k]
			U.N. system	Other			
—	X		5	0	2	8	2
13	X	X	14	0	4	12	12
—			13	1	0	17	3
92	X	X	17	3	57	45	42
51	X	X	17	3	19	24	10
17	X	X	15	1	11	28	4
6,372 (1,536)	131	125	2,087	243	3,311	4,080	2,995

[k] For a list of the forty-five selected international conferences, see Table 10.

[l] The United States and the People's Republic of China exchange liaison offices rather than regular diplomatic missions.

[m] Missions temporarily in the care of diplomats accredited to the United Nations.

[n] The two Vietnams were combined as the Socialist Republic of Vietnam in July 1976.

Source: Independence and area: U.S. Department of State, *Status of the World's Nations* (Washington, D.C.: Government Printing Office, Department of State Publication 8735, 1973), supplemented with U.S. Department of State, *ISSUES: World Data Handbook* (Washington, D.C.: Government Printing Office, Department of State Publication 8665, 1972), with updating. Population: United Nations, *Statistical Yearbook 1974* (1975), supplemented with *Status of the World's Nations.* Diplomatic Missions: *The Statesman's Year Book, 1975-1976* (1975), except the United States, which is based on a separate column of U.S. missions. U.S. Missions: U.S. Department of State, *Foreign Service List,* August 1975. Diplomatic Missions to U.S.: U.S. Department of State, *Diplomatic List,* November 1975. International Organization Membership: U.S. Department of State, *Treaties in Force, January 1, 1975,* but updated to January 1976 for the United Nations and the International Court of Justice. Treaties: U.S. Department of State, *Treaties in Force, January 1, 1975.* Tabulations do not include some forty-six bilateral treaties of the United States with eight former states and other entities, including three Baltic states (Estonia, Latvia, and Lithuania), three of the European principalities (Liechtenstein, Monaco, and San Marino), the Ryukyu Islands, and Brunei. International Conferences: U.S. Department of State, *Participation of the United States Government in International Conferences,* annual reports for 1945-1946 to 1959-1960; Department of State individual conference reports for 1943-1945; *United Nations Yearbook* for conferences in 1961-1972; and Department of State Conference Division files.

Appendix B

POTENTIAL ADDITIONS TO COMMUNITY OF NATIONS

	Islands	Square Miles	Population[a]	Category[b]	Dependency of
WESTERN HEMISPHERE					
Anguilla	*	35	6,000	A	United Kingdom
Antigua	*	171	70,000	A	United Kingdom
Belize (British Honduras)		8,866	120,000	B	United Kingdom
Bermuda	*	21	52,500	A	United Kingdom
Cape Breton	*	3,970	167,000	B	Canada
Cayman Islands	*	93	10,500	A	United Kingdom
Corn Islands	*	4	1,900	A	Nicaragua[c]
Dominica	*	290	70,500	A	United Kingdom
Falkland Islands (Malvinas)	*	6,430	2,200	A	United Kingdom
Galapagos Islands	*	2,868	3,100	A	Ecuador
Guadeloupe	*	686	312,500	C	France
Guiana, French		35,135	44,500	A	France
Kodiak	*	3,670	9,500	A	United States
Margarita	*	619	120,000	B	Venezuela
Martinique	*	431	320,000	C	France
Montserrat	*	32	11,500	A	United Kingdom
Navassa	*	2	Uninhabited	0	United States
Netherlands Antilles[d]	*	317	189,000	B	Netherlands
Newfoundland	*	43,359	522,000	C	Canada
Panama Canal Zone		553	44,000	A	U.S. administration

145

Appendix B (continued)

	Islands	Square Miles	Population[a]	Category[b]	Dependency of
Puerto Rico	*	3,435	2,712,000	D	United States
St. Barthelemy	*	40	2,400	A	France
St. Kitts and Nevis	*	83	58,000	A	United Kingdom
St. Lucia	*	238	99,500	A	United Kingdom
St. Pierre and Miquelon	*	93	5,200	A	France
St. Vincent	*	250	89,000	A	United Kingdom
Swan Islands	*	4	Uninhabited	O	United States
Tierra del Fuego	*	18,800	14,000	A	Argentina/Chile
Turks and Caicos	*	166	5,600	A	United Kingdom
Virgin Islands, British	*	50	9,700	A	United Kingdom
Virgin Islands, U.S.	*	133	62,500	A	United States
EUROPE					
Andorra		180	5,700	A	Quasi-independent[e]
Azores	*	904	291,000	B	Portugal
Capri	*	4	9,000	A	Italy
Channel Islands Guernsey Jersey	*	75	123,000	B	United Kingdom
Corfu (Kerkyra)	*	246	93,000	A	Greece
Corsica	*	3,369	270,000	B	France
Crete	*	3,207	456,500	C	Greece
Dodecanese[f]	*	1,044	54,000	A	Greece
Elba	*	87	30,000	A	Italy

		Area	Population		Sovereign
Estonia		17,410	1,418,000	D	U.S.S.R.
Faroe Islands	*	540	37,000	A	Denmark
Gibraltar		2	27,000	A	United Kingdom
Latvia		25,590	2,450,000	D	U.S.S.R.
Liechtenstein		61	21,500	A	Quasi-independent
Lithuania		25,170	3,300,000	D	U.S.S.R.
Majorca (Mallorca)	*	1,352	363,000	C	Spain
Man, Isle of	*	227	56,500	A	United Kingdom
Minorca (Menorca)	*	264	43,000	A	Spain
Monaco		0.8	23,000	A	Quasi-independent
Saar		991	1,112,000	D	West Germany
San Marino		24	12,000	A	Quasi-independent
Sardinia	*	9,194	1,474,000	D	Italy
Sicily	*	9,817	4,681,000	D	Italy
MIDEAST AND NORTH AFRICA					
Canary Islands	*	2,808	1,138,000	D	Spain
Ifni		740	53,000	A	Morocco g
Madeira	*	307	253,000	B	Portugal
Spanish North African Presidios		14	166,000	B	Spain
SUB-SAHARAN AFRICA					
Afars and Issas (French Somaliland)		8,996	81,000	A	France
Ascension	*	34	480	A	United Kingdom
St. Helena	*	153	4,700	A	United Kingdom

Appendix B (continued)

	Islands	Square Miles	Population[a]	Category[b]	Dependency of
South-West Africa (Namibia)		318,261	526,000	C	South Africa
Rhodesia, Southern		150,333	4,847,000	D	Declared independence (United Kingdom)
Zanzibar (and Pemba)	*	640	355,000	C	Tanzania
ASIA AND INDIAN OCEAN					
Andaman and Nicobar Islands	*	3,215	115,000	B	India
Brunei	*	2,226	136,500	B	United Kingdom
Goa		1,426	660,000	C	India
Hong Kong	*	398	3,948,000	D	United Kingdom
Kashmir		86,024	3,561,000	D	India and Pakistan
Kurile Islands	*	5,700	6,000	A	U.S.S.R.
Laccadive Islands (Lakshadweep)	*	11	32,000	A	India
Macao	*	6	248,500	B	Portugal
Manchuria		404,428	41,662,000	F	China
Mongolia, Inner		454,633	6,100,000	E	China
Paracel Islands	*	?	No permanent population	0	Disputed
Pescadores	*	50	108,000	B	Republic of China
Reunion	*	970	416,500	C	France
Ryukyu (Luchu) Islands[h]	*	848	1,120,500	D	Japan
Sakhalin	*	29,498	600,000	C	U.S.S.R.

Seychelles	*	52,500	A	United Kingdom (independent 1976)
Sikkim		205,000	B	India
Sinkiang (Turkestan)		635,800	4,874,000	D	China
Socotra	*	12,000	A	Yemen (Aden)
Spratly Islands	*	?	No permanent population	0	Disputed
Tibet		470,000	61,300,000	D	China
Timor, Portuguese (East)	*	7,332	610,500	C	Portugal (annexed by Indonesia, 1976)
West Irian (Western New Guinea)	*	159,334	923,500	C	Indonesia
OCEANIA				
Admiralty Islands[i]	*	800	23,000	A	Australia
Aleutian Islands	*	6,821	6,000	A	United States
American Samoa	*	76	27,000	A	United States
Ashmore and Cartier Islands	*	2	Uninhabited	0	Australia
Austral (Tubuai) Islands[j]	*	174	5,100	A	France
Baker, Howland, and Jarvis Islands[k]	*	3	Largely uninhabited	0	United States
Bonin Islands	*	40	200	A	Japan
Canton and Enderbury	*	27	Uninhabited	0	United States/United Kingdom
Caroline Islands[l]	*	463	56,000	A	United States
Christmas Island[k]	*	52	2,700	A	Australia
Cocos (Keeling) Islands	*	5	620	A	Australia
Cook Islands	*	93	21,500	A	New Zealand

149

Appendix B (continued)

	Islands	Square Miles	Population[a]	Category[b]	Dependency of
Coral Sea Islands	*	1	Uninhabited	0	Australia
Easter Island	*	64	1,000	A	Chile
Fanning Island[k]	*	13	376	A	United Kingdom
Gilbert and Ellice Islands	*	369	53,500	A	United Kingdom
Guam	*	209	85,000	A	United States
Hawaiian Islands	*	6,450	770,000	C	United States
Heard and McDonald Islands	*	113	Uninhabited	0	Australia
Johnston Atoll	*	1	1,000	A	United States
Kermadec Islands	*	13	Uninhabited	0	New Zealand
Mariana Islands[l]	*	184	14,400	A	United States
Marquesas Islands[j]	*	480	5,600	A	France
Marshall Islands[l]	*	70	25,000	A	United States
Midway	*	15	2,200	A	United States
New Britain[i]	*	14,600	166,000	B	Australia
New Caledonia	*	8,548	100,500	B	France
New Hebrides	*	5,700	78,000	A	United Kingdom/France— condominium
New Ireland[i]	*	2,800	50,500	A	Australia
Nieue Island	*	100	5,000	A	New Zealand
Norfolk Island	*	13	1,700	A	Australia
Palau (Pelew)[l]	*	184	12,500	A	United States
Palmyra Island[k]	*	1.5	No permanent population	0	United States

150

			Population		
Phoenix Islands	*	11	No permanent population	0	United Kingdom
Pitcairn	*	18	92	A	United Kingdom
Society Islands	*	150	21,000	A	France
Solomon Islands	*	11,500	161,000	B	United Kingdom
Swain's Island	*	2	100	A	United States
Tahiti	*	402	84,500	A	France
Tasmania	*	26,383	390,500	C	Australia
Tokelau (Union) Islands	*	4	1,600	A	New Zealand
Tuamotu (Paumotu) Archipelago[j]	*	330	6,700	A	France
Volcano Islands	*	8	1,200	A	Japan
Wake	*	2	1,600	A	United States
Wallis and Futuna	*	106	8,500	A	France
Washington Island[k]	*	5	450	A	United Kingdom
POLAR REGIONS					
ANTARCTIC					
Antarctica		5,100,000	No permanent population	0	Unpossessed—contested[m]
Bouvet Island	*	22	No permanent population	0	Norway
Crozet Archipelago	*	116	No permanent population	0	France
Kerguelen Archipelago	*	2,700	No permanent population	0	France
Peter I Island	*	97	Uninhabited	0	Norway
South Georgia Islands[n]	*	1,450	22	A	United Kingdom

Appendix B (continued)

	Islands	Square Miles	Population [a]	Category [b]	Dependency of
South Sandwich Islands [n]	*	130	Uninhabited	0	United Kingdom
South Shetland Islands [n]	*	?	Uninhabited	0	United Kingdom
ARCTIC					
Franz Joseph Land (Fridtjof Nansen Land)	*	6,400	No permanent population	0	U.S.S.R.
Greenland	*	840,000	48,500	A	Denmark
Jan Mayen	*	144	No permanent population	0	Norway
New Siberian Islands	*	11,000	No permanent population	0	U.S.S.R.
Northwest Territories	*	1,253,438	23,000	A	Canada
Axel Heiberg Island					
Baffin Island					
Banks Island					
Bathurst Island					
Cornwallis Island					
Devon Island					
Ellesmere Island					
Melville Island					
Prince of Wales Island					
Somerset Island					
Southampton Island					
Victoria Island					

Novaya Zemlya	*	31,900	No permanent population	0	U.S.S.R.
Severnaya Zemlya	*	14,300	No permanent population	0	U.S.S.R.
Spitsbergen (Svalbard)	*	23,957	3,500	A	Norway
Wrangel Island	*	2,800	Small	0	U.S.S.R.

a Population rounded to closest 500; under 10,000 figures rounded to closest 100; under 1,000 precise figures given.

b For population categories, see p. 18.

c Leased by the United States from Nicaragua in 1914 for 99 years, but terminated in 1970.

d Includes Aruba, Bonair, Curaçao, Saba, St. Eustacius, and St. Maarten.

e Condominium—France and Bishop of Urgel.

f Includes Rhodes.

g Spanish enclave ceded to Morocco in 1969.

h Includes Okinawa Islands.

i Bismarck Archipelago.

j French Polynesia.

k Line Islands.

l Micronesia; Mariana Islands opted for commonwealth status with United States in 1976.

m Sectoral claims have been made by Argentina, Australia, Chile, France, Norway, New Zealand, and the United Kingdom, which have not been recognized by the United States, nor has the United States made a sectoral claim.

n Falkland Islands dependency.

Source: United Nations, Statistical Yearbook, 1974 (1975), Table 18; U.S. Department of State, Status of the World's Nations (Washington, D.C.: Government Printing Office, Department of State Publication 8735, 1973); U.S. Department of State, ISSUES: World Data Handbook (Washington, D.C.: Government Printing Office, 1972); and The Statesman's Year Book, 1975-1976 (1975).

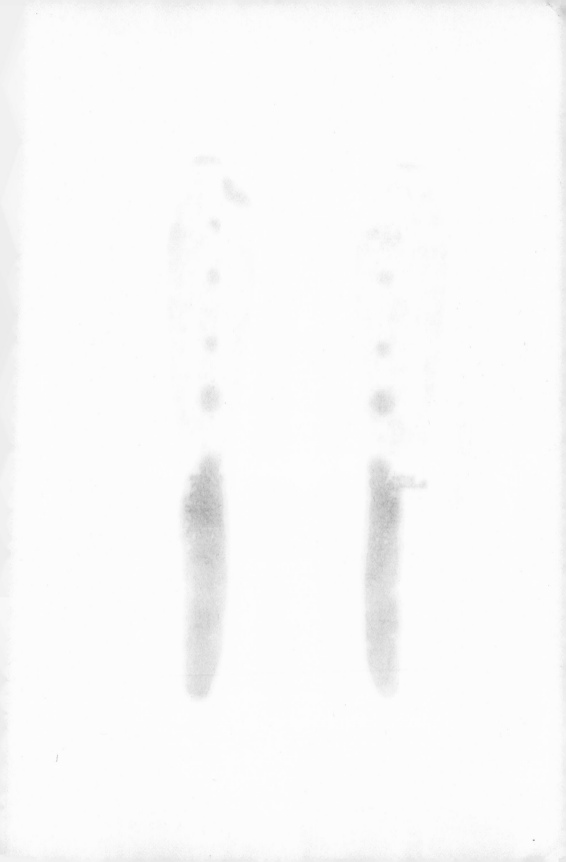

DATE DUE

Cover and book design: Pat Taylor